# THE ORIGIN OF SPEECH

# THE ORIGIN OF SPEECH

*Eugen Rosenstock-Huessy*

INTRODUCTION BY

HAROLD M. STAHMER

ARGO BOOKS

NORWICH, VERMONT

FIRST EDITION

---

Library of Congress Cataloging in Publication Data
Rosenstock-Huessy, Eugen, 1888-1973.
    The origin of speech.

    Based in part on: Die Sprache des Menschengeschlechts.
    Bibliography: p.
    Includes index.
    1. Language and languages – Origin – Addresses, essays,
lectures. 2. Languages – Philosophy – Addresses, essays, lectures. I. Title.
P116.R67  1981              401'.9              81-20527
ISBN 0-912148-13-6 (pbk.)                       AACR2

# Contents

# Introduction

The title of one of his recent works, *I Am an Impure Thinker* (1970), may serve as a portent of what to expect when reading Rosenstock-Huessy for the first time. For the initial reaction of many to his writings is frequently a mixture of fascination, exasperation and, occasionally, disbelief. In his foreword to that work, W.H.Auden warned ". . . anyone reading him for the first time . . . may find as I did, certain aspects of Rosenstock-Huessy's writings a bit hard to take." He then went on to add, "But let the reader persevere, and he will find, as I did, that he is richly rewarded. . . . The author's claim is just: he *has* uncovered many truths hidden from his predecessors." Auden concluded his remarks by saying, "Speaking for myself, I can only say that, by listening to Rosenstock-Huessy, *I* have been changed." I should like to second these sentiments. My first introduction to Rosentock-Huessy was as an undergraduate in one of his courses in 1948. Now, 33 years later, I still experience many of the feelings I felt then as a sophomore in his class. In the same breath I must add that of all the writings of great men that I have studied none has had as profound an influence on my life as have those of this "impure thinker."

Eugen Rosenstock-Huessy (1888-1973) was forty-five years of age when he left Germany for America in 1933. His wife, Margrit, and their twelve year old son, Hans, went to Switzerland and then, assisted by Henry Copley Greene, Rosalind Greene, and Mary Henderson, joined Rosenstock-Huessy a year later. Although relatively unknown in this country, in Europe his more than 150 books and articles dating from 1910 had earned him the respect of scholars in the fields of law, history, political science, and sociology. His friend and admirer, the political scientist, Carl J. Friedrich, negotiated an appointment for him at Harvard, but after two years in Cambridge he accepted an invitation to join the Dartmouth faculty as Professor of Social Philosophy, a position he held until his retirement in 1957. He died at his home, Four Wells, in Norwich, Vermont in 1973.

The appearance in 1938 of *Out of Revolution: Autobiography of Western Man*, introduced him to his American and English speaking readers. This was followed by *The Christian Future: or the Modern Mind Outrun* (1946), *The Multiformity of Man* (1948), *The Driving Power of Western Civilization* (1949), *Judaism Despite Christianity: The "Letters on Christianity and Judaism" between Eugen Rosenstock-Huessy and Franz Rosenzweig* (1969), *I Am an Impure Thinker* (1970), and *Speech and Reality* (1970). *Magna Carta Latina* (1974), *The Fruit of Lips or Why Four Gospels* (1978), and *Planetary Service: A Way Into the Third Millennium* (1978) appeared posthumously.

His English speaking admirers are representative of the "multiform character" or Renaissance quality of his thought and include, to mention but a few, Lewis Mumford, W.H. Auden, Reinhold Niebuhr, Abraham Joshua Heschel, Alexander Altmann, Nahum N. Glatzer, Dorothy Emmet, Maurice Friedman, George Allen Morgan, Page Smith, Harvey Cox, Martin Marty, Harold Berman, Richard Shaull, and Walter J. Ong, S.J.

*The Origin of Speech* is the eleventh work of Rosenstock-Huessy's to appear in English and, despite its compact size, may well be regarded by his American readers as one of his most significant statements. By way of background, most of the sections in this work were written in English during the war years of 1941-1945. When the German publisher, Lambert Schneider, agreed to publish his principal writings on speech and language in two volumes (1900 pages) entitled *Die Sprache des Menschengeschlechts* (*The Speech of Mankind*) (1964), Rosenstock-Huessy translated and, in many instances, drastically revised his unedited original English manuscript for inclusion in the German edition which appears, however, not with the original English title, "Origin of Speech", but rather with the title, *"Im Prägstock eines Menschenschlags oder der tägliche Ursprung der Sprache."* In many ways the German title is a more appropriate one considering the contents of the work; but unfortunately, it is difficult to translate into English. One possible literal translation is, "In the coining stamp of types of men or the daily origin of speech." But *"Menschenschlag"* can also mean "kind" or "race of men" and *". . . tägliche Ursprung der Sprache"* can also be translated "the periodic renewal of speech." Of all possible titles, I like best the one suggested by my colleague, George Morgan, "How Speech Coins Man," because it conveys the sense that we are "coined" in the sense of being shaped, impressed or stamped by speech which indicates to the reader the wide range of topics covered in this work.

The reader should be reminded that it was the intention of those responsible for the publication of this work that as little editing as possible be done in order to preserve not only the original format but its style as well. In this connection, it should be repeated that Rosenstock-Huessy did not edit or polish the style of the original English manuscript as was the case, for example, with the essays in *I Am an Impure Thinker* and *Speech and Reality*. When it was determined that an English edition should be made available, the decision was made to publish the original as it appeared in English rather than to work from the revised and more polished German version. One benefit of this procedure is that Section Six, "Logic on Trial," is included since it appeared in the original English manuscript but does not appear in the German edition. This section, now divided into seven subtitles, is the longest and accounts for a fourth of the entire manuscript. It should also be noted that the original manuscript did not include the kind of appropriate conclusion one is accustomed to in most of Rosenstock-Huessy's other writings. His son, Dr. Hans Rosenstock Huessy, Professor of Psychiatry at the University of Vermont College of Medicine, has therefore provided us with a brief concluding summary statement. Dr. Huessy also supervised the editing of the manuscript with assistance from Dr. Konrad von Moltke and Clinton C. Gardner.

One reason why *The Origin of Speech* is one of Rosenstock-Huessy's more important statements to appear in English is that it goes to the heart of his lifelong love affair with language; with grammar and speech, and in a most remarkable way serves as an excellent vehicle for understanding many of the key elements that have played so dominant a role in one form or another in almost everyone of his major writings. The key elements referred to are "speech-thinking" (*Sprachdenken*), his "grammatical method," the "Cross of Reality" (*Kreuz der Wirklichkeit*), his preoccupation with "time", his attack on Descartes' "I think therefore I am" (*Cogito ergo sum*) and, finally, the centrality of God in his writings.

Quite frequently students ask, "How do I begin to gain an insight into the meaning and structure of Professor Rosenstock-Huessy's thought? Which of his works in English should I read first?" In my opinion, *The Origin of*

*Speech* will serve as an excellent primer for future students asking such questions. It will also, I am certain, become essential reading for those already familiar with most of Rosenstock-Huessy's earlier published works because of the way it relates and ties together the above mentioned themes that are treated more extensively in his other writings.

It was apparent to Rosenstock-Huessy at age fourteen that language in the shape of philology, grammar, and speech had a special meaning for him. In a lengthy autobiographical essay (published as *Ja und Nein* in 1968), Rosenstock-Huessy stated that "from 1902 to 1942, *speech* made me the footstool of its new articulation .... Since 1902 I have lived consciously under the banner of *speech*." When in 1914 he published his major contribution in the field of law, *Königshaus und Stämme in Deutschland zwischen 911 und 1250*, he declared to his readers that *law* and *history* are intimately bound up with *speech*. He chose two mottos for that work, the first from Socrates, the second from Goethe and said, "The two mottos which preface a book on jurisprudence will, better than my assertion, prove to the reader that *language*, listening and speaking, have been my Alpha and Omega." This conviction had already been tested and confirmed in his famous encounter with Franz Rosenzweig on the evening of July 7, 1913. In his comments on their meeting, Alexander Altmann noted that "The 'philosophy of speech,' which was later to play so great a part in Rosenzweig's own thinking, had already been conceived by Rosenstock, ... at the time the two met in Leipzig (1913)."

When he was awarded an honorary doctorate in theology from the University of Münster in 1959, Rosenstock-Huessy was befittingly hailed as the New Magician of the North *(Magus des Nordens)*, the J.G. Hamann (1730-1788) of the twentieth century.

It is interesting that it was Hamann who was so critical of his friend, Johann Gottfried von Herder's (1744-1803) prize essay "A Treatise on the Origin of Language" (1771). Hamann charged Herder with having succumbed to the rationalist tendencies of his age by rejecting the higher hypothesis — namely, that speech was of Divine origin. Before he died in 1788, one hundred years before Rosenstock-Huessy was born, Hamann had written: "I speak neither of physics nor of theology; with me language is the mother of reason and revelation, its Alpha and Omega . . . With me the question is not so much: What is reason? but rather: What is language?"

Compare these words with Rosenstock-Huessy's:

> "And this temporal character of my thinking is in fact the Alpha and Omega from which I grasp everything afresh. Speech reflects this mode of procedure, even for someone who has been influenced by philosophy. For that reason I prefer to talk about speech rather than reason."

Readers unfamiliar with Rosenstock-Huessy's writings on speech and language may find the following comments instructive before turning to *The Origin of Speech*. First, while it is true that Rosenstock-Huessy is an "existential" thinker, his primary interest is *not* with the problems of authentic "individual" existence or *Existenz* (Jaspers); i.e. with evil, or with personal sin, guilt, or alienation, themes central to existentialists whether of the Kierkegaardean, Jasperian, or Heideggerian varieties. Rosenstock-Huessy begins not with the "individual" whether it be the sinner before his Maker, or the solitary thinker or solitary speaker, but rather with time and history, with the language of tribes and nations that empower and endow individuals to speak and thereby create new societies in time and space. Thus his comment, "Language is wiser than the one who speaks it." Or, as he wrote in 1912: "The living language of people always overpowers the thinking of individual man who assumes that he could master it." It is in this sense that "speech coins man." His "grammatical method" which is central to *The Origin of Speech* (Cf. also "In Defense of the Grammatical Method", Chapter One in *Speech and Reality*) should be seen against this background. His "speech-thinking" *(Sprachdenken)* is the active or "existential" form of "grammatical thinking". The reader may be interested in knowing that Franz Rosenzweig adopted Rosenstock-Huessy's method of "speech thinking" for his *Star of Redemption* (1921) and his essay, "The New Thinking" (1925) after reading Rosenstock-Huessy's "speech letter" to him in the winter of 1916. (Cf. Rosenstock-Huessy's *Angewandte Seelenkunde* (1916 and 1923). In "The New Thinking" Rosenzweig said that ". . . . the method of speech replaces the method of thinking maintained in all earlier philosophies. Thinking is timeless and wants to be timeless. . . . Speech is bound to time and nourished by time, and it neither can nor wants to abandon this element."

Rosenstock-Huessy's "Cross of Reality" (*Kreuz der Wirklichkeit*), which should not be confused with the Christian symbol, represents the temporal and spatial as well as the historical and social articulation of his "grammatical" method.

> "The grammatical method is the way in which man becomes conscious of his place in history (backward), world (outward), society (inward), and destiny (forward). The grammatical method is, then, an additional development of speech itself; for, speech . . . (gave) man this direction and orientation about his place in the universe through the ages." ("In Defense of the Grammatical Method," *Speech and Reality, p. 18.)*

"Grammar," for Rosenstock-Huessy, "is the future organon of social research" (*Ibid.*, p. 9). It's "existential" impact upon the "individual" who stands and lives "under the banner of speech" is captured in his motto, "I respond *although* I will be changed!" (*Respondeo etsi mutabor!*), "a vital word alters life's course and life outruns the already present death." (*Out of Revolution*, p. 753. Cf. the entire chapter, "Farewell to Descartes," pp. 740-753.)

As an undergraduate I was overwhelmed in class one day by Rosenstock-Huessy's declaration that "Man is a moment in time!" At age nineteen I had never really had a feeling for the meaning of time as he used the term. And being at least fifteen years away from Sputnik the term space was equally meaningless to me. Whenever I read him I am struck by the centrality of "time" in his thought and *The Origin of Speech* crystalizes yet another dimension of this in his rejection of the commonly held assumption that "The child is father of the man!" This theme is developed in Section Three in his discussion of the "grave as the womb of time." "The solidarity of man is created by transforming death into birth; and it was done by building tombs as the womb of time." This statement follows that powerful assertion of his, "The origin of human speaking is the speaking of human origin."

The other theme so central to this work and to all his writings is his assertion that real thinking is not an original or solitary activity, that speech precedes thought, that "you" (or "Thou") and not "I" is the historic grammatical first person. We think because we have been addressed, whether it be through song, lullaby, command, or confrontation. This thesis is the cornerstone of his "grammatical method" and enables one to understand his frequent allusion to the "time cup" of Man and how "reflection" and thought are related to speech which is the subject of Section Five.

In one sense, *The Origin of Speech* can be viewed as a sequel to the last chapter in his *Out of Revolution*, entitled "Farewell to Descartes"; in another sense *The Origin of Speech* not only attacks Descartes' *"Cogito ergo sum!"* but the older Hellenistic Alexandrian school's assumptions about logic and grammar as well. What he wrote in 1938 in that Chapter sets the tone for what the reader may expect when venturing into *The Origin of Speech*:

> ". . . The *Cogito ergo sum* tends to destroy the guiding imperatives of the good life. We do not exist because we think. Man is the son of God and not brought into being by thinking. We are called into society by a mighty entreaty, "Who art thou, man, that I should care for thee?" And long before our intelligence can help us the new-born individual survives this tremendous question by his naive faith in the love of his elders. We grow into society on faith, listening to all kinds of human imperatives. Later we stammer and stutter, nations and individuals alike, in the effort to justify our existence by responding to the call."

And finally, should Rosenstock-Huessy be considered a "theologian" or a "religious thinker", two appellations that he rejected with scorn repeatedly during his lifetime? "God", for Rosenstock-Huessy, "...is the power which makes us speak. He puts words of life on our lips." (*The Christian Future*.) In *The Origin of Speech*, he reiterates this point, "The very name of God means: 'he who speaketh; He who enthuses man so that man speaketh'." (Section One) His thinking can be described as "Johannine" in a millenarian sense in which the first thousand years are Petrine, the second thousand, Pauline, and the third and present, Johannine, or the Age of the Spirit that is dominated by the Word made flesh that dwells within us and "enthuses man." If he is, as some would describe him, a "pioneering religious thinker," then he certainly would make a very uncomfortable bedfellow who would kick, turn, and protest at the thought of being grouped among "death of God" or "liberation theology" types, to mention but two recent schools. Read his *The Origin of Speech* and try to resist the normal temptation to pigeonhole or type him. It is a most refreshing experience especially for those of us who tend professionally to equate meaning and value with typologies and generalizations. Rosenstock-Huessy breathes, speaks, and sparkles best when you allow yourself to come under his spell if only for a short period.

HAROLD M. STAHMER

Gainesville, Florida
October, 1981

# THE ORIGIN OF SPEECH

The origin of language is one of the most debated and most ridiculed and most hopeless questions of human history. It has been rejected as a wrong question which never can be answered and therefore never should be asked. It has been explained by "imitation," by nervous reflexes (Langer), as gesticulations of the whole body curtailed into a movement of the throat (Jousse), as the shouting of a warfaring group; and all these explanations border on the scurrilous. Most people acquainted with the treatment of the question are rightly discouraged.

The "origin" of language, to my mind, is as legitimate a question as any question of "origin." This means that it shares the one central limitation of all these questions: we must know what we mean by "origin," what we mean by "origin" of speech. Speech may mean:

A. A method of showing a man the direction to the next farm on the road or a way of stopping a child from crying. Then it comes in with gestures, smiles, and tears, and then the apes and the nightingales are our masters. There is no doubt in my mind that, in our daily chatter and prattle, our speech serves the same purposes as animal sounds. And things which serve the same function should be related. There are areas in our life where we share the conditions under which animals emit sounds of courtship, warning, etc. When we use sounds in these same areas they bear some resemblance to the languages sounded by animals.

B. But speech may also signify the power to sing a chorale, to stage tragedy, to enact laws, to compose verse, to say grace, to take an oath, to confess one's sins, to file a complaint, to write a biography, to make a report, to solve an algebraic problem, to baptize a child, to sign a marriage contract, to bury one's father.

Most people confuse A and B. They seem to think that by explaining lullabies and neighborly advice or chatting we also have explained the power of an oath. We are going to disentangle A speech and B speech from this confusion. Our confidence in dealing with the problem of speech is based precisely on the discovery that a nursery rhyme, a pointing towards the next house and the humming curiosity of gossiping neighbors have no right to pose as pretypifying human speech at all.

## 1. The Authentic Moment of Speech

It is easy to distinguish between animal sounds, formal speech, and informal speech. The question "How do I get to Tipperary?" and a lullaby and the nicknames of Jim and Jack are neither animal nor formal speech. They are "informal." In the United States everybody likes to be informal; informality is considered a great virtue. It is the goal of the good life to slap the President on the back and to call Eleanor Roosevelt "Eleanor." When "informal" is an ideal, it also seems to be normal. But we do more honor to our ideals by admitting that they take an effort. Informality is a rebellion against formality. Never can "informal" be called pre-formal. That would take the edge off. After forms have been created and perhaps grown stale, we may become informal. To be informal means to neglect forms which exist. That which does not exist cannot be neglected. He who likes to live and speak without formalities has not explained the birth of these same formalities. The situation brings to mind the case of an agnostic who sent his son to an orthodox minister for religious instruction. The minister asked the father if this was not perhaps an oversight. No, said the father. "After all, a man must have something to liberalize upon." The low brow must have something high brow to speak lowly about. Formalities explain our craving for the informal, not vice versa. Nobody, then, could speak and say, "Gosh, what a fine day" unless somebody had sung before, "the heavens declare the glories of God." Nobody could say *Mommy* or *Daddy* unless somebody had spoken reverently *Father* and *Mother* before.

The distinction divides all forms of speech into two halves which are in

constant competition: the formal and the informal. Logically and historically, the formal precedes the informal, and it succeeds animal speech. In an-
ticipation of our result, we may say 1. pre-formal animal speech, 2. formal
human speech, 3. informal, low brow speech. Informal speech capitalizes on
both the pre-formal and the formal; it is a compound of both.

Our distinction opens the road to a new investigation of speech: some
kind of speech exists with the animals. The human historian need not explain it; it is natural. Another kind of speech exists with man only. This
must be understood or human history remains a mystery. The acts listed
above as some acts of formal speech, from chorale to peace treaty, actually
constitute humanity in distinction from animals. But humanity caters to
lowliness and relaxation. Any formal speech is melted down until it is
liquified into informal speech between "cat and dog, *frère et cochon,*" as in the
nursery or the soldier's barracks. What we do to formal speech in breaking
it down to tidbits of information, informalities and innuendos cannot serve
to explain formal speech. In fact, it shows the tendency of absorbing,
obliterating, and levelling it. It is humorous, casual, unobtrusive, and
deprecating. Therefore we must forget all our informal habits when we wish
to understand the sublimity, elation, exultation, gravity, and precariousness
which it takes to speak formally.

Formal speech cannot have originated with groups whose whole bent is
to live informally. The mother-child relation, for instance, has to be excluded from the area in which formal speech might have originated. A herd or a
gang of youngsters or soldiers or hunters also is no environment in which
human formal language can ever have been born. It is in these environments
that science has looked for evidence. But the truth about them is plain.
These environments tear down all articulate or formal speech. They destroy
grammatical endings, they live by exclamation marks and the shrugging of
shoulders. They ruin the best language. What a strange expectation that the
wealth of forms in grammar and syntax could go back to a milieu that per se
is hostile to forms. Can a chemical agent which dissolves be used to explain
crystallisation? Can the informal slang of a gang explain the crystals of grammatical, formal speech? But this has been done, time and again, by
linguistics and by philosophers of language. Two trains of thought have
prevailed. Either one is struck by the fact that animals speak — under this
impression, the abyss between animal language and human language

becomes a mere ditch of negligible depth. Or we admit that speech should be explained in terms of human history. If this were the starting point, it might seem permissible to concentrate on children. However, the most unhistorical forms of human existence are children and their mother or boys in their gang. When we fix attention on these most natural groups among us, we assign to them the task of having created the most unnatural thing in the world, articulate and grammatical speech. We may, fortunately, look in the opposite direction, away from ape and from babies and boys and girls. When we search to understand the origin of formal speech it must be from a man's work or an old man's deed.

By changing the direction of our investigation radically and by looking in the opposite direction, we run the risk of going too fast. Child psychology and animal sociology are going forward among us with ever-increasing investment of capital and equipment and personnel. These vested interests will not admit, for a long time, that they are given to secondary studies in the realm of articulated speech, that their training has not prepared them for research in the fields of religion, language, politics, law, poetry, and ritual. They of course resent this suggestion that the child does not explain the man but, perhaps, the man the child.

Results alone can decide whose method is more adapted to the material which asks for interpretation. To find the origin of formal speech this book invites the reader to look at the attitudes of mature, grown up and responsible people among ourselves, to consider the acts of the wisest and greatest souls of all times. The results will be as simple as they will contradict the current prejudices. Speech is not a manufactured tool or a toy of our mind.

We may now sum up. We shall distinguish a sequence of three manners of social sounds between animated beings.

1. Pre-formal
2. Formal
3. Informal language

The sounds of animals are eloquent but pre-grammatical. Man's speech is articulate and grammatical. Children speak informally, dialectically, slang. From here we may go further. Man's language aims at something not aimed at by apes or nightingales: it intends to form the listener into a being which did not exist before he was spoken to. Human speech is formative and it is for this reason that it has become explicit and grammatical. Grammatical forms and names may be called the symptoms which prove that animal speech is superseded by articulate human language. This language can name a place Tipperary in Ireland, and a child Dorothy, the gift of God. This animals cannot do.

The greatest forms of man's speech are names. They clearly are not in animal language. Whatever man has in common with the apes when he speaks, the apes cannot call on God. The very name of God means: "he who speaketh; he who enthuses man so that man speaketh." So much did formal language long for names to which man should listen and in whose power he should speak.

If formal speech is particularly strong in names, formal speech may be labelled nominal or naming speech. This has some merits. By calling man's speech nominal, we gain access to one of the strangest phenomena of speech, the use of pronouns. *You (thou), I, my, we, that, it* are the most frequent words of a language. But they are used instead of names — *pronomine.* Instead of the term "table," we point to it as *it* or *that.* We must explain the distinction of name and pronoun; therefore we shall now replace the list preformal, formal, informal, by the terms pre-nominal, nominal, and pronominal. We shall call the languages of apes, birds, etc., prenominal languages, languages without names. The languages of humans we shall call nominal languages. Now comes our difficulty.

The areas of animal language between male and female, mare and colt, in a pack of wolves or chamois also extend into our own human relations. A mother and her children, a lover and his coy mistress, an officer and his men live in situations not completely different from the animal kingdom. It would be false pride to overlook the similarities of intimate comradeship which exist.

When formal language originated, the animated groups which correspond to animal groups found themselves between two influences: one the prenominal, preformal situation of the direct, physically visible and audible group of mates, of packs, of hen and chickens; the other the formal, grammatical, articulate language of names and places. The family, the platoon, the couple struck and strike a compromise between formal and preformal language: they speak informally. *Mommy, Daddy, Jim* and *John* are informalities. They are products of a grinding process between the two millstones of our animal and of our formative nature. Any word spoken in the nursery is a compromise between pre-formal and formal speech: it is informal. Logically, then, the informal is later than the preformal and the formal. It is their synthesis or mixture. It follows that *Mommy* and *Daddy* cannot be used to explain the origin of speech. Neither can my gesture, "There is your way to Tipperary" explain man's power to call the place "Tipperary" or to ask the question: "Which is the road to it?" *Where, your, which, it* are informal words which can be spoken because people meet as intimately as animals. In such intimacy, we need less formal speech than ordinarily. *Where, your, which* and *it* correspond to *Daddy, Mommy,* and *Johnny.* All these words are of the same character: small currency used in transactions of the moment. They are the copper one cent pieces compared to the formalities of a check or a war bond. Money experts will not understand money by meditating over the one cent coin only. One cent is too clearly a mere fraction of the dollar. The copper is a compromise between a short-term and intimate situation of two neighbors and the long-term and formal situation of the Federal Bank.

For this reason, *where, your, which, it,* are called pronouns. These words replace formal nouns. Similarly coins may take the place of "real" money. If we now extend the term pro-noun to words like *Daddy, Mommy* and *Johnny,* the whole relation of ape, man and child stands revealed. The ape in us speaks prenominally, the man in us speaks by names, and the child in us speaks in pronouns.

Prenominal, nominal and pro-nominal language are clearly distinguishable. Wherever people room and board and work and play together, in one place at the same time, they live in a pre-formal, more precisely, a prenominal situation. They can, therefore, get quite far by signs and sounds as the animals do.

On the other hand, lullabies, nursery rhymes, gossip, prattle, whisper, propaganda, jokes, puns, sales talks, advertisements and soap operas are not quite pre-formal. They are only informal. They are torn between the requirements of formality and common sense. They constitute the realm of the prounoun. They empty names by pointing, hinting and suggesting. A friend of my student days in Heidelberg invariably used the term "anyhow" (*irgendwie*) for all the mysteries of life. We decided that he used the term instead of the name of God. And so it was, indeed. Where former generations had spoken of the will or the help of God, he was satisfied with this uncertain and unspecified gesture of "anyhow."

Nicknames, short forms, pronouns and gestures, all abbreviate, empty and cheapen. But they render a positive service too. They protect names from wearing thin. The very vain Kuno Fischer, a German professor of philosophy, bore the formidable title of Your Excellency with great pride. However, one evening a young student at his house outdid himself in the use of the title. It rained "Your Excellency." Whereupon Fischer finally said: "Don't say it so often, young man. Once in a while is enough." In the intervals he was satisfied with the simple pronoun "you," instead of the full title!

Pronouns protect names in places and at times where their use is not authentic! We who look for the authentic place of speech by now have found the authentic place of pronominal speech: where formal speech is out of place, pronouns enter.

Pronouns are not animal speech. They keep a clear connection with the great names and titles of man's speech. *It, he* and *me* are full of form; *Daddy* is articulate and remotely refers to *Father*. Pronouns are less full than names; they protect the fullness by omitting most of the content. For the last 200 years people doing research on the origin of speech have not distinguished full and emptied speech. By lumping together lullaby and decree, gossip and oath, in one and the same category, we erect an insurmountable barrier against our understanding of the origin of speech. It is truly astounding how many problems become simple once lullabies are put in their proper place, in the nursery, and gossip in its proper place, in the parlor. Neither nurseries nor parlors are the fountainheads of formal language. The greatest victims of this fallacy were the names of the Gods themselves. People began to call God an idea. But ideas cannot be Gods. Names can. The nursery and the parlor presuppose the meeting house and the court and the formal languages spoken there.

Now, with the permanent obstruction by child language out of the way, we may well inquire when and where formal language is called forth, and what constitutes the contribution of language in a hitherto speechless community. The authentic place and the legitimate moment for the birth of language can now be explored.

Until we have faced the situations of a human society when and where speech is lacking we cannot even understand the second question of why the instruments of language were cast in grammatical forms. The question of the origin of language makes sense as a sequence of two questions. First, when, in our own experience, is new speech indispensable? Second, when, then, did speech become indispensable? Without any present day experience of speech as originating anew under our noses, from necessity, we shall have no yardstick for the past. Sceptics will say: this annihilates the question. There is no new speech today. Artificial languages offer no interest for our problem. Esperanto certainly does not explain Greek. Basic English does not explain Anglo-Saxon.

They are right. That which creates speech is not at work in these willful plans of speechifiers. But the sceptics are not right in every sense. History is not simply a matter of ten thousand years back. Pre-history is among us. Although artificial languages are not instructive for the origin of language, pre-linguistic situations in our midst do exist. These pre-linguistic or prehistoric situations reflect, to a measure, the field of force in which the first language originated. The vacuum is composed of the same polarities here and there. In each instance a pre-linguistic or preformal situation craves or calls for becoming articulate. Human beings as well as social conditions are waiting to become articulate. There is among us a muteness which waits to become speech. In asking ourselves where we don't or can't speak although we should speak, we may discover that function which is actually fulfilled by speech. We shall be outside of mere theory and we shall not abstract what language is from our little knowledge of English or German or Latin.

We shall try to learn from the sickness of a group which lacks speech why the health of a group depends on the origin of speech in its midst. We shall study the field within which the spark of speech is emitted before we study language. This negative approach to speech will put our debate of its origin on the firm basis of our own present-day experience. If a certain quality of life is impossible without speech, then speech should originate as restoring or creating this very quality. A comparison with other fields of knowledge will encourage us in our method. Economics became a science only when it began to study the crises in which the order of economics was destroyed. The eternal "origin" of economics, its perpetual bursting forth as an efficient division of labor, becomes understandable when we focus our attention on the disorder which arises from the absence of an efficient division of labor. Medicine is a science in so far as it penetrates into the mystery of disease.

Sociology becomes a science in so far as it can explain wars and revolutions. The absence of the proper order, the improper, serves to explain the "origin" of the proper order. When we have learned why one state of affairs is negative, and no good, we begin to understand the origin of the good.

Biology will be the science of life on that very day when death is fully understood. In the same sense we shall have a science of speech or of language as soon as we have penetrated the hell of non-speech.

In plunging into the darkness in which man cannot yet speak or no longer does speak to his brother man today, we shall prepare ourselves best for the answer to the questions: what is speech?, how does it originate?, why do we speak?, which, of course, are one and the same question in its divers aspects.

We are, then, going to inquire under what conditions modern man is not on speaking terms with his brother. This obviously is not a purely linguistic or philological question. If members of a family are not on speaking terms, something is wrong with the family. A moral question is implied. When nations are not on speaking terms, they are at war. It may not be a shooting war. But with Spain, Argentina and other countries we have made the startling discovery that a state may not shoot and yet be at war with another by not being on speaking terms with it.

Our way of putting the question for the origin of language shifts the field of the question into the realm of politics and history. The question "when must man come to speak?" is disclosed as a question which must have been answered by other authorities than the teachers of English or Arabic or Sanscrit. They deal with languages as facts. Our question deals with languages as question marks of political history. We wish to warn any purely literary or grammatical reader to leave us right here. For he will be disappointed when he finds that new speech is not created by thinkers or poets but by great and massive political calamities and religious upheavals.

Our question, then, is prephilological and prelinguistic. For this reason, our new way of asking eliminates a series of answers in which the last generation has taken delight or interest. These answers were based on the study of child psychology. Children were observed in their attempts to speak. And the origin of speech was explained in terms of these observations. Also, lunatics were objects of such observation. These psychological approaches are eliminated by our manner of stating the question. No child founds communities properly speaking. It learns languages which exist and operate. This is precisely the opposite from our problem of understanding what happens when a language is not functioning. I shall not exclude, at this point of our discussion, that children's genius may regenerate a community in which there is too little speech. The enfant terrible is as real as any genius. And children sometimes act as beneficially as adults. But my point is this: whenever children do regenerate a group which is failing in speech, they act like any founder or creator of speech in general. No difference can be made between young and old in this respect. It is then the saving grace of a child's word, not child psychology, which explains the origin of this word. It is a general quality common to all humans which is here evidenced in a child. Children per se do not invent speech, but they may act like full members who put the whole group right. This is the meaning of the truth: "out of the mouth of babes and sucklings, we shall find speech reborn."

Where, then, do we feel threatened and saddened by the absence of speech in our own life? There is not simply one fundamental situation in which man and man are not on speaking terms. The negative aspect of lack of speech is not sufficiently grasped in simple statements like: "The younger generation of whites and blacks in the South no longer speak to each other"; "You can't do business with Hitler"; "My parents are so old-fashioned that they don't understand me at all"; "The soldiers at the front don't understand the striking workers at home."

When we analyze these statements, the negative "no speech" splits into many "Nos" with different meanings. All these meanings are instructive. All should contribute an element of truth to our effort to find by induction what speech is and how it originates.

## 2. *The Four Diseases of Speech*

The various "No's" of speech point to the different functions of speech which usually keep a speaking unit together. An analysis of the divers "lacks" of speech is not as subjective or arbitrary as the reader might suspect. His suspicion was quite justified as long as all linguistic processes like the origin of speech were pigeonholed in linguistics. But we are treating the lack of speech as a political phenomenon of today. And as soon as one does this, one discovers to one's amazement that the peoples have long ago given names to "speech-lacking" ways of life. There is, in the first place, war. Peoples at war do not call the same thing good and evil. The one's victory is the other's defeat. Secrecy must shroud each party's plans. In former times, even the names of the tribes and the gods were kept so secret that the enemy could never impair their power by shameless perusal of these sacred names. The true and secret name of the city of Rome was kept as a secret in the temple of Vesta.

War, then, limits speech to the fighting group on one side. War draws a geographical line between two idioms. Also, historically speaking, war may produce a rift inside a linguistic unit. Civil war prepares the ground for a dualism of speech. English speaking South Africans speak more English English than the Canadians on the American border. The people in Chicago speak more American and less English than the Canadians.

But let us put aside Civil War for the moment and concentrate on war itself. A war ends when people begin to speak to each other again. Where this does not happen, war is latent still. A peace treaty is the beginning of speech between territorial neighbors. People who live in adjacent regions may be neither at war nor at peace. In antiquity this probably was the rule between the scattered tribes and countries. Today this state of indifference is exceptional. However, against this background, war is better understood. War is not peace, but it is more than the accident of coexistence in two adjacent areas without any contact or relation.

We may learn from war that groups may be not merely at war or at peace with each other but in a pre-relation state in which they have nothing to say to each other. In this state they simply don't exist for each other. Hence, no common values have to be expressed. War is different. Here the fact that people are not speaking to each other has come to a head and has led to an outbreak of violence. The intention is to come to terms of some kind. The peace is going to make law between the warring parties. Either one side is wiped out so completely that their speech disappears or a treaty and pact of peace establishes a common law. Then a new speaking unit comprising both armies is born.

War, then, for the ancients was not simply the absence or breakdown of peace as it is for us. For an abundance of cases existed in which people had withdrawn from each other and were scattered all over the globe. War was already one step toward each other, and the conflict, although an affliction, also was an action towards a peace. Life prefers suffering to indifference. War followed the absence of relations and was the conflict for the establishment of relations. Like any birth, the peaces had to go through the travail of birth called war. For our analysis it is well to keep in mind this background of indifference as a cause of war. The relations of the Red Indian to the whites were obviously of this ancient character. A distinct state of no common speech had preceded the state of belligerency. Today the Indian wars may be seen as the inevitable birth throes of the getting together of White and Red. War is the occasion at which the fact that neighbors in space are not on speaking terms with each other becomes intolerable.

A revolution is a break in speech also. But it is not a break between neighbors in space. A revolution does not listen to the old language of law and order. It creates a new language. This is quite literally true. Trotsky could write that the Russian Revolution had instituted a number of new worldwide words like Soviet, Kolkhoz, etc., and had killed others. A charming American book was written on the new language of the French Revolution. (This event created the adjective "revolutionary," for example.) Within barely ten years, the French language was changed, and even its pronunciation. The court's way of speech no longer made law. *Roi* and *moi* had been pronounced in the manner of our pronunciation of "loyal" and "royal." After 1789 the Parisian pronunciation of *Roa* and *loa* was victorious.

But a revolution is inarticulate at first. In war both warring parties have their sets of language. Two languages which exist clash. In a revolution the revolutionary language is not yet in existence. Revolutionaries are called young for this very reason. Their language must be grown in the process of the revolution. We might even call a revolution the birth of a new language. And as such all the great revolutions of the West are treated in my books on revolution. Here we shall advance to a definition of revolution in comparison with war. In a revolution old speech is rejected by a new shout which struggles to become articulate. The revolutionaries make a terrific noise but nine tenths of their whoops will evaporate and the final language spoken by the bourgeoisie or the proletarians thirty years later will have been cleared of these shouts of the beginning. But during the revolution suffering results from this very fact that the revolution still is inarticulate. The conflict lies between an over-articulate but dead old language and an an inarticulate new life. War is conflict between here and there, the languages of friend and foe, revolution conflict between old and new, between the languages of yesterday and tomorrow, with the language group of tomorrow attacking.

Two more conflicts exist. The opposite of revolution is tyranny or counterrevolution. In a counterrevolution the old attack the young, and yesterday murders tomorrow; yesterday is attacking. Its technique is significant. While the young revolutionary group shouts because it is still inarticulate, any reactionary counterrevolution is so hyperarticulate as to become hypocritical. The disease of reaction is hypocrisy. Law and order are on everybody's lips even where circumstances of a different truth prevail. Trusts and monopolies call themselves free enterprise. Unions cartellizing labor speak of freedom of contract. Decadent families speak of the family's splendor and claims to privilege, and so on.

Since war and revolution are more readily studied among us than the two other negative situations of speech, it must be emphasized that the tyranny of the old is as real as the violence of a powerful neighbor in wartimes, or the violence of the young in times of revolution. The tyranny of old age leads to degeneracy. No children are born, no future is envisaged, small communities dwindle. No new enterprises of small size originate any more. The sources of new life dry up. The small town is still cited as the home of all the virtues. But this lipservice does not induce anybody to live in such a small town all the year round. The family is idealized in sermons and editorials. But people in this same degenerating civilization may marry on a purely temporary basis and remain unencumbered by offspring. The term "marriage" simply grows hollow. And so it goes with patriotism, freedom, etc.

Lipservice is the cause of tyranny. An old order is degenerate, abusing future life wherever lipservice takes the place of shouting. The equilibrium between yesterday and tomorrow consists of an interplay between articulate namedness and inarticulate unknown-ness. I who am anonymous today must and desire to be known and make a name for myself tomorrow. If society is so "cliché," so clogged that it won't let my day arrive ever, it has degenerated. If speech is unable to be reborn sufficiently, speech is absent between old renowned life and new unknown life.

The facts of "lipservice" under the tyranny of the old and of wild shouting under the tyranny of revolution show up the social diseases of decay and revolution as diseases of speech or language. They illuminate the linguistic problem of war, too. In war both groups shout across the trenches and across the words of propaganda, but inside they are fully articulate. The trouble in war, then, is that speech is meant to be true in a limited area only: I tell you the truth, my friend, but together we lie to our foe. The trouble with war, then, is the regional character of truth. I do not believe what the enemy says. Whatever he says, I make war on him. Victory in war means not to have listened to the enemy! We may define war, in terms of speech, as a situation in which we won't listen to the enemy but are very sensitive to any rumor or whisper inside our own group. To sum up:

| | | |
|---|---|---|
| war | hypersensitized to words spoken inside | immune to words from the outside |
| revolution | hypersensitized to shouts of the young | immune against the old slogans and laws of old |
| degeneration (tyranny) | lipservice to old stock phrases | immune against inarticulate new life |

We now have reached the point where we can determine a fourth disease of communal speech. As revolution and counterrevolution balance each other, so war has its counterpart. It is possible to be immune against words spoken "inside" my society. If we look for the best term for such a situation, we may use tentatively the words crisis or anarchy. When an unemployed person knocks at my door, and I say: No work for you, no linguistic problem seems to be implied. Yet, it is. The unemployed person who asks for "work" actually asks to be told what to do. I am inclined to think that our economists overlook the stringency of this claim as a claim to be spoken to! We wish to be told what to do in society. The inner crisis of a disintegrating society is constituted by the fact that too many people inside this society are not told what to do.

It is hard to understand for most people today that this should be a disease of speech. They all are accustomed to think of speech as an utterance of thoughts or ideas. Thus, when an unemployed businessman tries to get an order in, or an unemployed worker hopes for a job, the connection between this demand and speech is overlooked. However, speech, in the first place, is orders given. When parents decline to give orders to their children, the family ceases to be a family. It becomes a bundle of ill-assorted individuals. Orders are the sentences out of which any order is composed. The abstract use of the word "order" has made us forget that "law and order" are the sum of all the imperatives and orders given over a long period of time.

An unemployed man is a person who looks for orders and can't find anybody to give him orders. Why does he look for them? Because orders fulfilled give rights. If I make a figure of clay, I have no claim to make money with it. But when I am ordered to make figures of clay, I establish a claim. Responses to orders given establish rights. The millions of unemployed during the thirties hoped to hear somebody telling them what to do. Precisely the opposite discrepancy exists in war. In war we won't listen to the enemy. In crisis we can't find anybody to tell us. In war there is too little willingness to listen; in crisis too few people are willing to give orders, to speak with the original power of speech, with the power of direction.

The list of elementary speech diseases is now complete. We shall analyze it with regard to the question of why it is complete and then proceed to state the lesson implied in these diseases for the normal and healthy state of speech.

> War: not listening to what the foe says
> Crisis: not telling the friend what to do
> Revolution: inarticulate shouting
> Degeneration: hypocritical repetition

Speech includes listening and speaking, articulating and repeating. A healthy speaking group uses old terms for new facts (repetition), new terms for old facts (articulation), spreads out to new people (speaking) and includes every worthwhile speaker (listening). The two acts of listening and speaking constantly extend the territorial frontiers of speech. We want to be able to speak to all and to listen to all. The two acts of repeating and articulating constantly extend the temporal frontiers of speech. We want to link up with all past and future generations.

All four acts are fraught with risk. More often than not they miscarry. War, revolution, decadence, crisis are the four forms of miscarriage. In war people who think we should listen to them are excluded; in crisis people who think we should talk to them are not included. In revolution orders which expect to be honored are ridiculed. In degeneracy shouts which expect to be taken up remain inaudible.

> Deafness to the foe
> Muteness to the friend
> Shouting down old articulation
> Stereotyping new life

are war, crisis, revolution, decadence when analyzed as speech-diseases. As deafness, muteness, shouting and stereotype they bear names which clearly point to the circulation of speech.

The objection is legitimate that war is not deafness, crisis is not muteness, etc. Gunfire and torpedoes and bankruptcy and impoverishment are what they are, in themselves. They are great calamities, even catastrophes of gigantic dimensions. Is it not like shooting arrows at a battleship to call these catastrophes diseases of the circulation of speech? The symptoms of these outbreaks of social disorder and our diagnosis of a little lack in the vital flow of the "still small voice" look so disproportionate.

I certainly do not wish to detract from the awe produced by these convulsions. And I do not intend to suggest that we should not be overawed by apocalyptic events such as the 1929 crisis, the Bolshevik revolution, the World Wars or the fall of France.

But as to the diagnosis, I must stick to my guns. That the diagnosis is correct may be seen from the healing process. A war ends by the writing of a peace. A revolution ends in a new order of society. The fall of France is overcome by its vigorous resuscitation, and a crisis ends in a new confidence or in credit restored.

Now all these remedies are of a "linguistic" or grammatical nature. When peace is signed, peoples speak and listen to each other again. Rejuvenated France has become willing to admit new energies to her councils. The Bolshevik Revolution has created a new order which now treats as a first cause that which was previously merely the result of accidents in society: production. And the crisis of 1929 has given way to new types of credit. The confidence of the public had to be restored by these new types of credit. Peace, credit, social order, new council, all bear the connotation of grammatical elements and remedies introduced through a better set-up for the exchange of speech.

Peace makes us listen to our former enemy. Credit is our speaking response to the man who asks to be entrusted with a task. The new social order is the cooling off of the revolutionary fever and shouts of Bolshevism into highly articulate blueprints for daily routines. The representation of youth, of the Resistance Movement, prevents the return to the stereotype of the overaged Third Republic.

Let us confront disease and remedy:

1. War as deafness, to peace as willingness to listen.
2. Revolution as shouting, to order as ability to formulate.
3. Crisis as muteness, to credit as willingness to entrust.
4. Decadence as stereotype, to rejuvenation as new representatives.

When we make those confrontations, the apocalyptic catastrophes shrink to human dimensions. They are so anomalously big as long as the flow of speech remains clogged. When this flow circulates again, the size of our social environment suddenly ceases to be awe-inspiring. Where peace, credit, order and representation function well, we feel at home and in our appropriate dimensions. The world is neither too big nor too small in the plenitude of speech. Where the plenitude of speech dries up, we immediately experience a change in our sense of dimension. We are overwhelmed, overawed, overpowered. We compare the social catastrophes to earthquakes, floods and fires because we feel quite inadequate. In fact, we feel lost and small in a sea of troubles. Whenever speech sets in again things seem to be under control. We breathe calmly again, the storm has subsided. The ocean of tumultuous disorder has become a duckpond of peace.

Obviously the dimensions have not changed objectively. There are still the same 2 billion people on this planet. But since we now know how to speak to every one of them the over-dimension has vanished. Our voice masters the elements of society again. The fourfold "No" of speech constitutes the great social calamities of our own time. And in our own time they threaten us with annihilation unless new peace, new order, new representation, new credit make themselves heard.

We draw the conclusion that language serves the purposes of peace, order, representation and credit. The eternal origin of new speech is based on man's mortal danger from war, crisis, decay and revolution.

If this is true, the original character of all language should be connected with man's victory over these evils. And accordingly we shall proceed from here towards the analysis of language. If our diagnosis is correct, the structure of language should bear witness to its political purposes. Before turning to this investigation, one more question may be asked which still concerns our own present-day experience. Are any one of the four benefits instituted by new speech — peace, order, representation and credit — independent of each other? Is it meaningful to speak of war, crisis, revolution and decay as separate diseases? Are four separate speeches instituted, one to make peace, one to end the crisis, one to liquidate the revolution, and one to overcome decay? Obviously not.

If I credit a man with fifty thousand dollars, if you treat him as my trustee, if our sons respect our undertakings, and if we allow our children to marry outside our own environment, I, my debtor, you, our sons and our daughters-in-law — we all must speak one and the same language. However, the credit ended an economic disorder, your helping in my disposition showed that you and I are at peace, our sons show a law-abiding respect for their elders, and we show a healthy respect for the calls of new unsettled life.

War, crisis, revolution and degeneracy are lopsided diseases of one and the same body: speech. Speech that is not spoken everywhere results in war. Speech that is not spoken on all necessary avenues of life inside its own area results in crisis. Speech that was not spoken yesterday ends in revolution. Speech which cannot be spoken tomorrow brings decay.

Speech must operate on four paths of health lest it die. This is true in our own day, and it is true of all days of men. It is a timeless truth.

We now are equipped to look into the past. Speech was intended to make peace, to give credit, to respect the old and to free the next generation. Its forms must have served these purposes since without them any human group collapses. Since we have a human history of thousands of years, the power has been effective.

When we now look into the historical beginnings which saw men rise to peace, respect, freedom and trust by formal speech, one more barrier which separates us from this past deserves mentioning. Speech came before writing. Oral speech therefore had to accomplish that which we accomplish by the spoken and the written word together. Our whole civilization of written and spoken language must be put together on one side — peace treaties and Colonel House's talks, ordinances and election speeches, paternal sermons and the sheriff's summonses and the doctor's certificates, strike rumors and the miner's contracts — and should be compared with a tribe's initial oral language. The tribe's formal speech was word of mouth and "book in print" simultaneously. It was also song and speech, poetry and prose, in one. It was formal for the very reason that the formal and the informal speech, book and whisper, song and speech, prose and poetry, law and love, had not yet been divorced.

The formal speech of a tribe of "uncivilized" men could not run: "sugar daddy" and "what's up?" and "gosh," because it served the purposes of church and government in the oral state of these institutions. The authentic place of speech lies in moments where peace, order, credit and freedom are created. Such acts constitute man's humanity.

By looking into the present, we could see that catastrophes like the Bolshevik Revolution, the World Wars, the Great Depression, the fall of France, constitute speechlessness of one kind or another. The negatives were varied and specific, and by their concrete variety speech lost its pale and general character. Its peculiar energies appeared by which it constitutes society.

When we now look into the forms of speech in the past, we shall use a similar method. The negatives have clarified the positive qualities of speech which conquer all four diseases. The forms of tribal language will become transparent when we treat them as forms which bear relations to other forms of group life. The modern catastrophes explained to us the logic of language, its authentic purpose, its logical place as an answer to definite needs. Ritual and ceremonies do the same for us through history. By defining language as a social form among other forms of social behavior, it will be seen in its interrelation with other institutions. Because it interacts with other forms, it is not wholly responsible for our group life.

In Parts One and Two human formal speech has revealed itself as an answer to definite needs. In Part Three it remains to discover its own definitive properties, its own authentic form.

## 3. "Church and State" of Prehistoric Man

Our contribution to the task of defining the situation in which speech became formal and articulate is not based on mere speculation. The facts of pre-history and anthropology are unanimous. They go to prove that men used speech for construing an "in-between" situation between the grave of one generation and the initiation of the next. Speech created a field of force between those who had lived and those who were going to die. Usually we express this fact by admitting some relation between the dead and the living. We explain funeral ceremonies by saying that the dead were considered still alive. This is not the true faith of mankind. The faith of mankind reversed the relation of death and birth: the dead were worshipped insofar as they had lived as "precedent"; the living were emancipated insofar as they were ready to die as successors.

Peace and order depended on this reversal of the so-called natural order between birth and death. For the modern sophisticated and scientific mind, birth precedes death. "The child is father to the man," we say from this purely individualistic point of view. The individual considered as a unit from his own birth to his own death would have remained speechless. Animals, indeed, are speechless for the very reason that they are nobody's preceders or successors. The constitution of mankind consists of the establishment of the tomb as the womb. The tribes, the empires, the churches do not differ in this respect. Obviously, they used very different methods. And I would hesitate to say that the methods of our era are the "right" methods, and the methods of the tribes are obsolete. But this distinction is of secondary importance for us who wish to interpret grammatical speech.

The agreement between tribe and Church is complete with regard to the relation of us who are going to die and those who have lived before. This relationship in both cases is conceived as the opposite to the zoological. It denies man's zoological right of finding himself between birth and death. He is asked to realize himself between death and birth! Both tribe and church are at a loss to understand the method of science which arranges these occurrences as though birth precedes death. They both would say and do say: "This is blasphemy, it plumps man into the very state of 'dog eat dog' out of which tribes and the church, by their formal speech, extricated man."

If man reckons life from birth to death, progress is denied. Progress depends on the intersecting quality of death as the womb of time. Between grave and cradle, civilized man becomes articulate, becomes enlightened and finds orientation and direction. The pressures resulting from the grave produce the slope by which the waters of life can reach the heights of a new birth. The animal is born. But it cannot penetrate the time before its own birth. A dense curtain precludes its knowing of its antecedents.

Nobody tells the animal of its origin. But we, the churches and the tribes of time immemorial, have lifted all human beings from their dependence on mere birth. We have opened their eyes to their origins, to their predecessors. We have transformed their mere births so that they became a succession of precedents well-known and well-established. And we have transformed their mere deaths into a precedent leading to an emancipation of their successors. We have made men know their origins by originating one tongue for them. The origin of human speaking is the speaking of human origin! Speaking one tongue, men have become and can continue to become Man.

When I learned to speak of my origin, of the processes preceding my own birth, I acquired the power of bespeaking and betokening the processes succeeding my death. And these two powers of prescience before my birth and of determination after my life distinguish me from the animal. The origin of speech lets the "natural" relation of birth and death be superseded. The whole momentum of our train of speech is that of all speeches made, all songs sung, all laws enacted, all prayers prayed, all books written — every one is in the direction which makes death the precedent of birth.

It is easy to draw the distinction between natural individuals and historical "Man" when we observe by what procedure death is created into a precedent. The mere physical stopping of life belongs to the body which expires. But a burial, a funeral, a eulogy, an obituary, reverse this into a speech and a monument for the living. Now comes the stupendous fact: *there are no human beings who do not bury their dead.* In this one act, man conquered his own separateness, ceased to be an individual, and penetrated the cloud of his own blind existence by recognizing parents who begot him, whose life he is called to continue. When we speak of graves instead of death, we already are committed to this reversal of the "natural" order which man enacted ever since he first used formal language. The funeral is not an adaptation to nature. It is a complete revolution away from and beyond nature. It establishes knowledge of "each other," a brotherhood of man unknown in the animal kingdom.

The solidarity of man is created by transforming death into birth; and it was done by building tombs as the womb of time. On the other end of life, there is birth. Birth is any animal's fate. In itself it is not humanized; it has no special quality for man among other living creatures. But birth was transformed into its opposite, just as death was. There is no human group which does not initiate the young. The last relic of these universal proceedings is baptism. The parallel between funeral and baptism is precise. That which seems part of me is made an event in the life of other generations.

We have said that the grave is made the womb of time, and that the origin of speech is speaking of origin. Now we may add that the purpose of speech is speaking of goals. The initiate is told where he is going and learns to anticipate his death. He is asked to treat his life as though it already stretched out beyond his own death. He is given a name which shall survive his physical life. He is called to serve as a bridge into a time which is not measured in terms of his own physical existence. The grave as cradle corresponds to the coffin of all rites of initiation. Christian baptism holds on to this universal tradition. The child is made to die to this world even before it has lived in it and is called forth so that, by the very momentum of this call, it may push through this life into the state beyond the grave. Through the institutions of burial and initiation, the whole of our physical existence becomes transparent in reverse order. Burial is a second birth, setting the precedent; initiation is a first death, making man think of his need for successors.

Speech reverses the chaos of nature, the strife between mere individuals, its lack of continuity and of freedom. In nature every specimen is born by itself and dies by itself. Everything is necessary. Fate prevails. Speech creates peace, order, continuity and freedom. It gives man an office and a share of life by enlarging the notion of life. He is emancipated from thinking of himself as the yardstick of life. The very term "life" is the root of much evil in modern discussions. It is promiscuously used for denoting both individual life and the eternal life which tribesmen and churchmen experience in holding office and in sharing. Our modern sceptics borrow from the dignity of the terms "eternal life," "social life," "historical life," when they rave about "vitality" and "the rights of the living." Inextricably, in our thinking, the life of the race and the life of individuals are mixed up.

While our enthusiasts of pure nature adore the life force and the energies of nature with all the contrition of true worshippers, they naively expect all of us not to serve our own life, between our birth and our death. They expect all of us to listen to their sermons on nature's laws, to put the life of mankind above the life of the individual. They expect scientists to risk their lives in experiments, explorers to risk their lives in deserts, inventors to defy popular prejudice. In every instance these speakers in praise of nature assume that we will appropriate their point of view as the right and natural one. They live in the frail edifice created by our first ancestors with whose help man turned against nature and defied its chaos, its disorder, its necessity. The worshipers of human nature live with us in the very graveyard in which we have learned to worship at all. They exploit our capital of worshiping power, acquired when formal speech lifted the veil from our eyes about our origins and our destiny. But does it really make any difference whether we place ourselves between our own birth and death, or between death and birth? The modern mind is so sober that it still thinks primitive man was too superstitious, too afraid of death. He should have taken it easy, not expended all his fortune on funerals for his elders and not heaped all the cruelties of misfortune upon the poor initiated youngsters. If speech really enabled man to slaughter 300 captives and 100 horses, and to burn widows on the pyre, to tattoo faces and trunks and to circumcise and subincise the young, it seems to stand less justified than condemned.

Did the field of force established by the power to speak of origins and to betoken destiny really create peace and order, freedom and progress? Is there a universal proof for this?

No human being marries his own mother. There are limitations to marriage in every tribe or group we know of. Our latest literature, for the first time in the history of mankind, jogs this first result of revealed origins. Novelists and analysts question the rules of incest. We are told that the deeply buried instincts of daughters for their fathers, of sons for their mothers cannot be neglected, that their repression does harm to the "individual." All human society, indeed, has begun with the creation of islands of peace. From these islands of peace, warfare, jealousy, rape and anarchy were excluded. Peace was based on the exclusion of sexual competition. The most primitive group has found means of establishing peace between the sexes. Within this relationship the seasons of passion and of indifference can alternate without losing their togetherness. The forms of marriage may vary from polygamy to monogamy, from temporal to eternal vows. But no tribe of "savages" is without marriage.

Marriage means renunciation and it means distribution. The members of any family are constrained. The family, the island of peace, is castrated as such, is made chaste. The term chastity did not apply to an individual's morality, but to the mores within the family where sex was quieted and toned down. A family group was chaste when and insofar as incest did not occur. Chastity, then, is man's oldest term for peace. Such a peace did not come about by accident. Marriage is a fight against the natural events of incest. The tribe bought the peace of chaste groups by paying a price for this peace. It allotted to certain occasions and certain groups the liberty of sexual intercourse. No tribe without the dances of the group, the orgies between the sexes, the libertinage by which alone the chastity of each family could be adhered to.

In discussions on marriage, I nowhere find mentioned the simple fact that in primitive society any family left to its own decisions on chastity would have died out through child-incest. Nobody could think of demanding chastity from the smaller family group unless the larger group of the tribe compensated for this loss by sexual opportunity for the children of these families! The tribe instituted family chastity no less than funerals and initiations. This peace divided the blind life of the sexes into places of chastity and places of animality. The orgies of the tribes do not deserve the label obscene or lascivious or profligate; on the other hand, they cannot be passed off lightly either. Like all prostitution they are the price paid for the peace of the family — as St. Augustine in his Academica well knew. Every peace costs a certain price, its toll to the chaos of nature. The peace of the family is built on this price of promiscuity on the tribe's holidays. In fact, the division of man's seasons into holidays and ordinary times is based on this necessity for peace in the family and equivalent orgies outside. The calendar of all groups of men distinguished festivals and work days, not by accident. Men recognized themselves as brothers and sisters only by cutting out islands of peace (families) and by meeting each other outside these islands, occasionally. These indispensable occasions are their festivals.

Marriage, then, is the organization of life between chastity and orgy. Marriage is not understandable per se. It is one pole in the alternating organization of a tribe. In the family the young people do not mix sexually at will; on holidays they have occasion to do so. The family tones down, the holiday keys up. Without this frame of reference of the tribe, the family cannot preserve its features. The breaking up of our present day family results from the very fact that this polarity is gone. When men are expected to be chaste "per se," incest becomes a grave problem. The rhythm is upset by which we first created a truce, some kind of peace, between mother and son, father and daughter, brother and sister, partly because the orgies which balanced this peace are disintegrating.

The islands of chastity veiled man's and woman's eyes to their mutual sexual attractiveness. And they did this, among other things, by bestowing titles on the inhabitant of these islands. The great names of the family, father, mother, brother and sister bear a remarkable feature: they are formed in their endings like the words "other" and "better." Cuny, a French linguist, has drawn attention to this little symptom. The analogy with our words for comparisons, our ending in "er" for any comparative (long-er, strong-er), seems to show that they were conceived not only as pairs but as more intimately, even conditioning "each other." Only where there is a father can there be a mother, strictly speaking. A mare has colts. A woman may have offspring. These acts do not make her into a mother in the full sense of this term, in antiquity. Motherhood is too plainly a title for an office than that it could be acquired before our era by unmarried women. The interaction of "father" and "mother," "sister" and "brother," is a constant problem for all of us. This is best shown when divorces became rampant and children began to see their parents as individuals again, as male and female. The constitution of the family forbade this distinction to the children. Parents were conceived of as being in office, as Lord and Lady. Their relations as sex partners were made secondary. Children must not conceive of their parents as sex partners in the first place. The very meaning of the family is destroyed if Johnnie calls his father the man who sleeps with Mommy. The names father and mother have exactly the purpose of reversing the situation in this respect. Bride and groom they are indeed. But to the rest of the world they are made apparent as husband and wife, and as father and mother.

Once more we encounter the obvious fact that all men at all times have abolished the laws of nature by decree and by name. When the bride is veiled, the rest of the world is forbidden to think of her as the bedfellow of such and such a man. She is his wife and therefore the natural is superseded by the unheard-of relation of husband and wife. In this relation the wife represents the husband and the husband represents the wife lest any trace of sexuality be left visible to children and neighbors. The man may bed down when his child is born. This famous ceremony is only one climax in this reversal of nature's law. The wife wields the keys in her husband's absence. She is like one of his children in Roman law which is but another way of signifying the chastity of her position. In our order, she bears his name, which tells the same story. They are one flesh, according to the Church, which again seals the covenant of peace above "individuality" or, better, their "dividedness." That a male and a female should escape the crude classification by sex and should be recognized by the community as husband and wife is the fruit of speech. It is utterly unnatural. It reveals a relation not given in nature but created by faith. The experiences of primitive society with regard to man's creative powers centered upon the grave, the cradle and the bed of marriage. Compared to our theology, his belief in the Gods may have been vague and shifting, but his belief in marriage was unshakable.

It is, however, much more difficult to believe in marriage than to believe in God. The destruction of the law of nature by which any man under sixty will try to seduce any woman under forty is an act which requires the same quality which the belief in Gods demands: it requires faith. Faith is our perpetual power of resisting specious argument and appearances. The argument that after all, male is male and female is female, is ready every morning and every evening, to any normal male and female. The world today is full of these arguments. Faith builds marriages against these arguments. No marriage can exist without this faith. And in the case of marriage, it is not the profession of this faith which counts, but its naive enactment. For this reason, we said that the belief in marriage is more difficult than the belief in God since "belief" usually is degraded to its statement in so many words.

If man and woman can become husband and wife, then daughters and sons will see in them their father and mother, and will, for this reason, treat each other as brother and sister as a reflection of their parents' chastity. A group which produces these fruits has reversed the course of nature. At a certain age, sex certainly is the strongest passion of man. But speech, by bestowing the title of husband and wife, has mastered nature. It revealed a new way of life to those who believed.

Marriage organizations form the heart of any primitive society. But why is marriage the fruit of the reversal, introduced by speech in man's relation to birth and death?

A Roman married *liberorum procreandorum causa*. The offspring is called *liberi* (*eleutheros* in Greek), a member of the coming generation. Freedom and marriage are reciprocal. Why are children born in wedlock "free," and most out of wedlock are not? This is yet another question utterly obscured by Rousseau's naturalism and his craving for foundlings. The only reason is that "free" means to have been foreseen as the coming generation, to have been expected and willed as potential successors. The parents have acted as preceders, not as genitors, but as "pro" genitors. The veil was lifted and they knew what they were doing when they begot these children.

Greek mythology and all myths of all peoples never tire of dwelling on the two ways of begetting offspring: the illegitimate and the legal. Nobody was naive enough to assume in those days that sexual intercourse was limited to married life. This absurd fiction belongs exclusively to our own times. But people felt that the competition between marriage and sex orgy was a real competition between faith and natural reason: faith establishing the peace of marriage, natural reason defending the brigandage of sex. The conflict of faith and reason is eternal. We disguise it into one between theology and science, in which form it loses all importance. But Zeus's illegitimate children and Hera's sponsorship of marriage were of the greatest social importance as everybody could see and grasp. The title of the free, of the "coming generation," could not be bestowed on those whose future was not hewn out by the older generation's voluntary restraint and opening up of their "coming." Future and freedom, liberty and "coming," are two aspects of the same thing. Without foresight no freedom. My father's foresight is my freedom. My own "future" is made possible by the love of the preceding generation.

In my youth I was told that the Roman marriage formula "*liberorum procreandorum causa*," "to call forth a free offspring" was terribly prosaic. We may now marry for love because we expect any number of public institutions from kindergarten to socialized medicine to take care of our brats. However, I can no longer be blind to the fact that each of these institutions originally was part of the family, including even medicine. Hence, every marriage meant the founding of a small nation with due respect for the freedom of its future citizens, the free and legitimate children. Parents sacrificed their lifetime and devoted their whole being to this founding act. No wonder that they acquired the titles of a new status as husband and wife; public law, not private contract, was the basis of marriage. And the sanctions had to be of a religious nature lest arbitrary tyrannical despotism suppressed the children. In other words, marriage was the mainstay of public law; this public law, in turn, was realized at the intersection of the death of one generation and the birth of the next. The vows at a wedding are not understood unless they are again placed in their authentic place. They were spoken because the new founders found themselves placed between preceders and successors, as a middle phase between ancestors and grandsons. Outside this chronological place, the vows could not have been spoken. Because their every word made them one phase in the voluntary connection between tomb and womb, an act of respect for tradition and for freedom simultaneously.

## 4. The Conflict of Political Sense and Common Sense

Any political structure, we now may conclude, takes human beings into times and spaces denied to their bodily senses. These times are larger than one individual lifetime and these spaces are wider than one individual can hold under his own power.

Every political order expands the time by which a person is limited and the space in which he is contained beyond his own life's "bournes." This expansion is "unnatural," "supernatural," "transcending." It does not happen automatically. It is established by man's devotion and dedication to this unforeseen and unpredictable task. Its permanence is never assured. Any political structure may collapse any moment unless its existence is renewed by the faith of men committed to it.

Formal speech is the means of establishing as well as of re-enacting. Formal speech nominates men to functions in a body politic. It invokes a common spirit in whose name all its members promise to serve and are promised to be served. It signifies objects of the outer world which shall serve the body politic as its natural basis. And it must initiate the "eleutheroi," the "liberi," the "up and coming," to enter voluntarily into this fragile and perpetually risky undertaking.

By formal speech, man emerges from chaos. Chaos is not simple but complex; its analysis helps to see the crucial task of society in its complexity. Chaos may annihilate the bonds of fellowship; it then becomes disorder or anarchy, from lack of credit. Chaos may annihilate vitality, from lack of freedom. It then becomes despotism and degeneracy by prejudice and stagnation. Chaos may annihilate continuity, from lack of respect; it then appears as rebellion and revolution. And finally, chaos may annihilate the laboriously established new "bournes" of the body politic; then it takes the ugly shape of war. But the names which denote social chaos are in themselves creations of formal speech. Men who had established peace before now are able to call war a process of attacking the established super-time and superspace of the tribe.

Some pacifists indulge in calling war murder. Ever since men could speak, murder and war stood approximately at opposite ends of the scale of social processes. The murderer was and is pre-tribal; he expresses his will against another will. War defends the order to which the warrior has surrendered part of his will because he believes in a higher, supernatural peace and order between men which depends for its existence on his acts. Not to go to war, means to desert the peace which my body politic has established. Not to murder means to respect the continuity which my body politic has built up.

The first body politic, the tribe, was built up as a peace between families. Families are subdivisions of a tribe. No family can exist outside the tribe. The corollary to the family's peace are the tribe's orgies and marriage classes. Logically, the "idea" of the tribe precedes the family. The convenient phrases in our textbooks that "families grew into tribes" need revision. They did not grow into tribes but originated from tribes. Because of the nominal and explicit high speech of the tribe, the family could achieve three ends:

1. Peace between sex rivals and punishment of offenders against chastity. The home acquires a sacred peace.
2. Peace between age groups, between the generations of men. Offenders of the spirit of tradition and respect are outlawed, become "wolves." They would leave the tribe, found a new one and create a new language.
3. Peace between the realm of the five senses and a hypersensuous political order of spaces and times quite out of the reach of any "individual."

These three goals are reached by devising for the home a place not growing out of "nature," but assigned to it in an explicit division of labor. The home receives an assignment under which its members hold office as one "fireplace" inside the superbody of the tribe. The tribe's ritual institutes each family as one of its centers of "common sense." Common sense relates to sense and high speech in the same manner as informal speech relates to preformal and to formal speech, as pronouns refer to the sounds of animals, on the one hand, and to the nouns of high speech, on the other. Common sense, nowadays, is not treated as an historical product. But common sense is the final product of the conflict between man's animal nature and the social roles conferred on him by names. At the fireplace of each family, the high speech of the tribal spirit is shaken down to the lowest denominator. Thereby it becomes common sense.

This common sense accepts the supernatural emergence of a family which has given up jealousy and rebellion and tyranny and murder, but in the shadow of the tribe's protection it takes its existence so much for granted that it need not use the big words and songs and incantations and oaths and curses spoken on the tribe's holidays. Common sense relies on this background. Where the tribe has to be explicit, any common sense group proceeds implicitly.

Everything in which we believe implicitly had to come into existence explicitly once. This, then, is the relation between common sense and pronouns and informal speech in the family on the one hand and super-sense, or political sense with the nouns and forms of the body politic on the other. One "sense" is not without the other. Rousseau's and Benjamin Franklin's craving for a human society of pure common sense is nonsensical. "Emile" and Poor Richard derive all their common sense as a precipitation of the political super-sense; the more common sense we have, the more political sense must we already have developed, and vice versa. The reason for this constant polarity is speech. Speech emerges not from common sense but from the founding fathers, the heroes who found a new structure. Common sense absorbs existing speech; it makes us at home in an existing political structure. We relax. But new speech is created under the pressure from graves in back of us and cradles ahead of us, from foes in front of us and dissension within our own ranks. These are situations sorely lacking in common sense, situations which cry out for explicitly conscious, most formal and most definitive statements.

The cry for peace and order is a desperate cry. Shouting for freedom and for regeneration of the good old days is of the utmost violence. The lullabies and sugar coating of common sense are not acceptable to crying, weeping, shouting, raging people. They must experience the miracle of seeing the dead come to life again, and foes become friends, and dissent become agreement, and shouts become new words. They must see and hear and touch before they believe. Formal speech produces exactly these miracles. The dead seem to come to life, shouts become prayers, foes come to terms; inner dissent becomes harmonious song of strophe and antistrophe, of dialogue and chorus.

If speech did not achieve these miracles for society, it would be unnecessary. As a "means of communication" it is only used by common sense. But 10,000 languages have been spoken over thousands of years just as often as means of excommunication as of communication. They have cursed the werewolf and the demon and the despot and the enemy just as often as they have blessed the child and invoked the spirit and obeyed the Lord and reconciled the enemy. Any tribe has been exposed to constant attack from within and without. Its formal language has kept it in existence as a body politic through migrations over the earth and over decimations and ravages through time. Miraculously, it is anchored in an eternity and defies space and time. Speech is the political constitution of a group beyond the life time and living space of any individual, beyond common sense and physical sense.

Our picture of the emergence of speech would be too rosy if we did not stress the imperfections of all tribal order. Greek mythology was mentioned before because of its open pessimism. Too many defied the tribe and did not bury their dead but slew the old men as hithertofore. Too many raped and violated the women. Too many did not come to the tribe's meetings. As in our own days, the social order was incomplete. The "Berserk" and the "Titans" were real. These men would rage, would not speak; they were breaking out from the tribe. These facts warn us against overrating the works and the creations of speech. If it had not failed time and again, we might think speech to be infallible. As a natural process, speech would be infallible. Most anthropologists are convinced of the natural character of speech. They never ask under what conditions it must function. In all their research, they naively presuppose that man first can speak and then goes into politics and "organizes" society. The opposite is true. Man must speak if he wishes to have a society; but very often he cannot speak and then his society breaks down. Supernatural processes are as often absent as they are enacted. We should hold our breath a minute and ask ourselves: Shall we be able to articulate our chaos into order once more? There is no guarantee for success since at no time has every tongue or every speaking group succeeded in provoking men to trust and freedom — some have, some have not. All speech must take the risk of being misunderstood by common sense. This risk is truly formidable. The whole untruth, fallacy, hypocrisy and lie of many social relations springs from this ineptitude of common sense to understand the full meaning of the great forms of language.

The father of lies, the devil, is nobody else but the community of common sense which always whispers and tells us: "so what?", or "say one thing and do the other," or "think one thought and teach another", "sell one idea and cherish another", "have one conviction in private and another conviction in public", etc. Nobody today believes in the existence of the devil because nobody thinks much of speech. In the District of Columbia, officials are required to take an oath for no other purpose than for getting their salary. The oath, then, is a farce. Now, the oath as administered in Washington, D.C., may be a farce; words may be empty of meaning. But the body politic must be able to speak with authority just the same. And a man must be able to pledge his very life for a sacred purpose.

When old forms are worn, men will not be at peace unless some ways of formulating new forms instill us with new faith and respect. The conflict between form and common sense leads to the diseases of speech. Diseases of speech make men into liars. A liar is a man to whom society gives a bad name. He believes not what he is supposed to believe. That may be the fault of society or it may be his fault. But such discrepancies invite disaster. These discrepancies have been created from time immemorial. We suffer from our own creations. Prometheus is not the only hero whose liver aches while his body is chained to the rock of time. Ever since man spoke he has been divided against himself. Only half of his speech is successful and fully understood. The other half is either dead wood, or it is betrayed. Pledges broken, credits abused, bank checks not covered, blue laws never obeyed, lipservices in prayer abound.

The true miracles of speech, as all miracles, are threatened by their false imitations. Every church has its agnostics next door; every true statement invites pseudo statements. In his speech at St. Andrews, Rudyard Kipling insisted that the first speaker was a liar. This could hardly be; but the second speaker probably was one.

We do not understand the history of either state or church through the ages if we do not recognize this unavoidable flaw in the very beginnings of articulate speech. The relation between truth and lie is the human problem brought on by our creation of human speech. As Clemenceau said in his contempt of man, "Only flowers do not lie." Neither do they speak except when we send them as words of our human language. But his word goes to show that man had to fight the father of lies from the beginning.

The earnestness of original speech, its formality and solemnity can only be appreciated by observers who sympathize with this tragic aspect of our aspirations. Our analysis of the forms of speech should be helped by our sense of danger, of possible betrayal which lurks in all speech.

## 5. Speech versus Reflection

We moderns are no longer afraid of the devil. The ancients were. And everything they said took this danger into account. For this reason the reflections of modern thinkers on the speech of ancient or primitive peoples are not valid. Dr. Sigmund Freud, or Mr. Linton or Mr. Malinowski or Mr. Rank or Mr. Wilhelm Schmidt reflect when they write their scientific books. To reflect means to be relatively safe. The authentic place for reflection is a time span of complete safety and relaxation. The authentic place for formal speech is a moment of chaos and highest tension, between the devil and the deep blue sea. This is, as we now see, quite literally true. The deep blue sea is the open unsettled chaos and the devil is the temptation to use stale words and incantations without meaning, without the will to act upon them.

Any American has access to this authentic place from his own history. "Four score and seven years ago, our forefathers proclaimed that men were born free and equal." For four score and seven years this incantation had been repeated but not acted upon in the South. In 1860, then, Americans were between the father of lies and the deep blue sea of trouble. The great name of "Mankind," used with "due respect" in 1776, by 1860 showed implications never dreamed of in the beginning. The name of Mankind, the terms "free" and "equal" used as the promise of a New World required that we should cash in on them by acts of faith.

This relation between Jefferson's Declaration of 1776 and Lincoln's Gettysburg address is a relation faced by any original group of common speech. Its names are promises to be acted upon. Christian and Hildegard and Frederic and Alfred and Dorothy and Faith and Grace and Hope are imperatives. They challenge their bearers to act upon the promise they contain. The so-called "theophoric" names which contained a god in their structure like Godefroy, Ramses, Thutmosis, Diodor, Thursday, Sunday and Friday were not statements of fact but promises and commands, invitations to the bearer and to the spirit invoked upon the bearer and to the community calling the bearer by this spirit's power.

The names of original speech all face in three directions: they face the public which is told, the person who is called, and the "spirit" which is invoked. Modern reflection classifies names as uniform concepts on which it can generalize. Linguists speak of "theophoric" names as a certain "class" of words. Psychoanalysts may classify them in the class of taboos. Historians may compare them to certain names of later phases — baker, miller, hunter — of a secular and professional character. Reflection treats words as simple and specific and generalizes upon them. The pathway of science leads from facts to generalization. Most educators think that the power of generalization is the best power of the mind.

Authentic speech cannot be classified as going from facts to generalizations; this is left to academic reflection. The abolitionists and the signers of the Declaration of Independence did not move in the realm of reflection or higher criticism. They spoke. And to speak is a communal commitment in three directions: I say; I am ready to be quoted on what I say; I insist that the thing I say has to be said.

Speech begins with every word spoken in good faith that it is true, that I will stand up for it under attack, and that I hope the rest of the community will believe I am telling the truth. It unfolds its historical life as an interaction, a drama between my belief in my people, my faith in the truth and my trust in myself. Every name spoken in its authentic place is an act of faith, of community, of obedience, of social interaction. Its whole power derives from its triplicity, and a name which no longer produces this tri-une current between the public, the speaker, and the inspiration, is dead and must be buried.

Our academic reflection on words and names does exactly this: it buries and analyzes dead names which no longer ignite the spark between speaker and listener and truth. Reflection is the gravedigger of past processes of speech. Its time comes after the authentic place of speech has been vacated. It then defines the word "Dorothy" as meaning "the gift of God." This definition is made outside the community where the name Dorothy grew out of a dangerous situation. Here was a clan with a tyrannical matriarchate, let us say. The name Dorothy was given to coerce the mother of the child; to tell the bloody tyrant the truth about her child: it was not hers but a free gift of God. The name was indeed a taboo; it was intended to protect the child against abuse by its parents, it was an amulet and a charm. But was it not also an obligation for Dorothy, a constant appeal to her sense of responsibility? And finally, what a fine praise of the Deity, what a submission to the creator of mankind? Any one of these "meanings" of the name "Dorothy" would suffice for its definition. But none of them makes sense outside the constant interaction between all three. The term "meaning," then, does not suffice to explain language. The meaning of meaning is not discovered by defining our terms. Our semanticists are alright when they apply their method to dead words of the past. They are gravediggers. They are quite helpless with regard to the names which still connect the semanticists themselves and their public in a spirit of cooperation and trust. A short reflection not on words of the past but on the names under which these semanticists act may prove this central point concerning all the misunderstandings about speech.

Our semanticists are called semanticists; Semantics is a science. We are expected to believe that there shall be science, and that it is a good thing to read the books on semantics written by scientists before we use our terms in public. The term "science," in this context, is not treated as a fact which exists, but as an act on which I, the reader of the scientific book, am expected to spend 10 dollars, and on which the writer stakes his reputation and his time. He is speaking to me in the name of the science of semantics. I submit to his speech on account of the authority which the name of science holds over me. Let us hope that he, the semanticist himself, does not abuse this authority for a hoax but that he will do as well as he possibly can. But how do I know? How can he himself know that he "is" scientific? Well, he has predecessors whose method has shown the path to truth; he follows their example. This is a great help. Also, he has been checked by fellows of the same profession. He may have a degree. This is help number two. Finally, he exposes himself to my finding out for myself in the wake of my reading his book and following it up. This is help number three in the defense of truth against hoax and abuses. These three remedies or defenses against the pseudoscientist constitute the perpetual defenses of society against pseudo speech:

> The speaker is a follower
> The speaker speaks in a fellowship
> The speaker is followed up

The semanticists are alive only in so far as their train of thought moves on the beaten track called science, is certified to contain real scientific ware by a fellowship of fellow scientists, and can be followed up by every critic and reader in a wide open and free public.

Take a speaker, instead, without contact with the achievements of science, without a reputation at risk, and without the authority of a lawgiver to his followers. The names of his books which he sells have no antecedents, no partners, no possible criticism. Hitler's *Mein Kampf* shows what must happen when scientists overlook the truly powerful interaction of spoken word, acting like a theophoric name by which the speaker and the public conspire and invoke a common spirit. There are, then, no other living names but "theophoric" ones; all names invoke a spirit of fellowship among followers of one and the same God. In our own time this fact is denied since the authentic place of speech is continuously confused with the place for reflection. As the gravedigger of words played out, reflection is not the midwife of living truth. The ancients were fully aware that a man had to prove himself a follower, a partner, or an author with every word he said, and that his name could be a harbinger of blessing or curse.

We must discard our own methods of speech in the reflective mood before we can understand the logic of language. The logic of language is built on a kind of knowledge which the modern scientific mind does not even consider as a remote possibility. The ancients knew that words are least misunderstood or betrayed or forgotten if they are not fully understood in the beginning. They allowed every word a long time to be heard and understood. They assumed that the speaker and the listener of high speech would slowly and gradually understand what had been spoken. The marriage vows — well it takes us a lifetime to know what we have vowed. Speech takes time before it is filled with meaning. Nobody expected from a hymn or an oath or a charm that it should be anything but a promise of gradual understanding. Names are not generalizations, as our philosophers think. Our ancestors considered generalizations pure deviltry. They would have judged it blasphemy to treat education as the power to make generalizations. Names, to the initiated adolescent were promises of a slow ascent to understanding. They were shrouded in mystery, not because they were not true but because they were meant to come true.

But how did they ever come to pass, these promising names? This is a very legitimate question. Obviously, the dignity of such names could not be based on some phonetic quality, on the imitation of the sounds of water or fire. True, some words of our language do depict natural sounds. But they are not at the core of human speech. At its core are names meant for long time attachment to lived lives of real people. The spirit of language and the language of the spirit are lived life condensed into names. "Spirit" is usually called the power of a name to contain past and broad realms of a life actually lived so these can be experienced by those who invoke that name. When we compare the figures ten or five or three with the names of Gods and men, the figures may help us to define the names by means of a contrast. Figures are understood without lapse of time. Hence, we have invented a special script for 1, 2, 3, 4, etc. Mathematics is the science of facts which requires no real living through time to be understood. But names are on the opposite pole. All men of all times must have lived before we shall know God. God is neither a figure nor a word. He has a name. All names other than the name of God are shortlived. But all of them demand to be filled with meaning over long periods of time. America was discovered in 1492, named in 1507 and it has been acquiring meaning year after year ever since. In this slow process, any interruption may ruin all the previous steps. Christianity can be made a fallacy by this very generation. For if it does not spread to Japan or return to Germany after this war, then, quite obviously, it has never been true before.

All speech is subject to abuse and misunderstanding because it appeals to perpetual following up. Authors, partners, followers are involved in speech. It either builds up a society or it dies. The miracle that we can speak at all seems to me at times far greater than its naturalness. And indeed, never was speech in greater danger than in the days of science when the indicative of "it rains," 2 + 2 = 4, the mood of reflection, are considered authentic speech. Alan Gardiner, famous Egyptologist, has written a book on the origin of language in which he begins by analyzing sentences like "it rains." This is a typical approach to the question because "reflection" prefers the reflective mood in speech. The indicatives of language are the concessions to the scientific or reflective mentality. Yes, we may say: "2 plus 2 is 4," we may say: "The Mississippi is the largest river in the United States." The librarian and archivist in my brain is welcome. He may have his say. He is the librarian and the statistician who takes stock of names spoken before in agony and hope, in despair and faith, from hate and from love. The indicative, however, is no indicator of the creative moods of language. Horace poked fun at this latecomer of life, who appears after everything has become a fact because it is over, in his *"Eheu fugaces, Postume, Postume, labuntur anni"* (Alas, in flight, you lateborn, lateborn, slip away the years). And the poem goes on to speak of all the "musts," all the future that no after-thought will stop from coming. The sentences are all built in the forms of prophecy (*erimus, absumet, sequetur*) or in the gerund, the form of commanding "there shall be' (*enaviganda, visendus, linquenda*). The reflective mood surveys facts which can be labelled and defined, and Horace makes fun of it.

## 6. Logic on Trial

In grammar this reflective mood is called the indicative, and the science of logic is built around it as though sentences which are put in the indicative are the normal sentences of a lived life. But man does not connect himself with the universe by sentences spoken in the indicative. The indicative "two and two equals four" serves a quite exceptional situation of speaker or listener. When neither the speaker nor the listener are in a position to alter a fact, they speak of it in the indicative. When I say, "He is dead", "Europe is a name of the past" or "The snow is three feet deep," I am saying that I cannot do anything about these things, people, and names. I am also saying to you that you have to accept these truths as facts. The indicative explicitly emancipates the minds of speaker and listener from their entanglement in that part of reality. It absolves them from any form of further participation except through the faculties of the mind. The indicative in "The snow is three feet deep" indicates that the snow is "mine" only by my knowing intellectually of its being three feet deep. The indicative stresses the looseness of my or your connection with the thing stated. It is a purely mental connection. The science of logic is not the science of all connections with reality. It is limited to purely mental connections.

It is an historical accident that this limitation was placed on the notion of what logic is. Logicians having declared speech to be illogical unless it is a mere statement of fact, it is only proper that we should look into the beginnings of logic and ask ourselves why when reflecting on speech they restricted the "true" moods of speech to statements of fact.

Logic began as the science of speech. Then in the last centuries before our era, it also described the material on which it was going to work. Grammatical forms of human utterance were sorted, and various classes of words were collected: nouns, pronouns, verbs, participles, infinitives, etc. Words were observed with regard to their position in sentences; and sentences, it became clear, were either main clauses or subordinate clauses. "Give answer lest I die," was a sentence composed of the main clause "give answer," and the subordinate clause "lest I die." All these distinctions were handed over to the grammarians. Logic then concentrated on the main clauses. The new science found that there were four forms of main clauses. It gave them names which we still use: "Give answer," was a sentence of command; "May I have an answer," was a subjunctive or optative sentence of wish; "You answered me," was narrative; the sentences "he answers" and "this is an answer" were indicatives. So far so good.

Now came the fateful accident. Fateful because it forever isolated Greek logic from Hindu, Chinese, Jewish and Egyptian traditions. The four sentences

| | |
|---|---|
| Give answer | Imperative |
| May I have an answer | Optative |
| You answered me | Narrative |
| This is an answer | Indicative |

are all main clauses. Grammatically they are all irreproachable. And they all make sense. A science of the meaning of speech could start with any one of them or, better still, with all four. They all describe pirouettes of our mind in making its statements about reality. When describing Greek logic, Maier, the author of the famous *Psychology of Emotional Thinking*, expressed amazement that one type of sentence — "This is an answer" — should have carried the day.[1] There is, indeed, no reason why "logic" should be based on this one form of sentence. Maier thought so and wrote on the optatives, subjunctives, etc., of the mind. This was forty years ago and a very exceptional step it was.

Maier, however, made his own choice without reference to a new frame of reference for all logic. He acquiesced in the precedence of the indicative and asked only for some place to which no such wishful thinking would be admitted.

This, however, once more left our occidental logic to accident. The sentences the Greeks blocked out are logical sentences; they were treated as dead ends. The entire truth concerning the human mind was expected from an analysis of sentences comprising mere statements of fact. Logicians did not reflect on human statements with vital meaning and significance. To the contrary, they reflected exclusively on reflecting statements! They never inquired if the proper place for reflecting statements could be explained in contradistinction to other statements. This "logic of the schools" resulted in a growing sterility of all the other processes of speech. The times of Alexandrian scholarship produced not one great poem, not one new prayer or law. The Church remedied this drought, again watering men's souls with the full power of speech. We need not go into the manner in which she did this. Anybody who reads the first chapter of Genesis or the last chapter of Revelation can test our assertion that Greek logic is discarded in favor of a logic in which all the sentences,

> Give answer
> May I have an answer
> You have answered me
> He answers

hold equal rank. Only the one form of sentence, "this is an answer," on which Greek logic had staked all its scientific research, was discarded by the Biblical thinkers.

By this one omission the connection between logic and Bible, between reason and faith, was obscured. Both seemed to speak of different processes:

one based truth on imperatives, optatives, narratives; the other on indicatives. And both stubbornly declined to compare notes. Hence theology is illogical to the logician. And the logician appears irreligious to the theologian. How absurd!

Obviously, nobody is justified in stigmatizing any legitimate form of speech by which we keep our social mills going. We have used them all from our childhood days, and they have been used for us ever since we were born. When we reflect on our mind, we find it stored with imperatives, songs, stories, rules and equations. All together they tell us what is in our mind, and one of them is not better than any other.

We therefore intend to go back to the first survey made by logic and reflect on all forms of independent sentences. Perhaps this reflection will enlighten us more about our mental processes than either logic or theology.

In the sentences,

> Give answer
> May I have an answer
> You have answered me
> He answers
> This sentence is an answer

there is one definite distinction between the first four and the last. The first four sentences express relations between listener, speaker and reality explicitly. The last one does this only by implication. "This is an answer," it is true, is pointedly said by somebody referring to something called "This" which he can indicate by a gesture. There must be a speaker and there must be a reader or a listener who can look at the same thing with him and speak of it as "this." But the form of the sentence does not explicitly show this fact. No you's, he's or I's appear in the sentence, and it appears to live regardless of any author or recipient. How do the other sentences fare in this respect? They all refer to the relation of the speaker, the listener or of both to the act itself.

Pre-Greek logic — or post-Greek logic if you like — has to make this central discovery: in all human sentences except in the indicative, the speaker or the listener are connected with the content of what is said in more than one way. They are not reduced to a pure mind which observes, but the very life of the act depends on their living as a part of it! This is true even of the apparent indicative, "he answers him." This sentence which is usually lumped together with "2 plus 2 is 4" and "this is an answer" as being of the same type, is really not a pure mental statement. The speaker can say this only in full truth if he is physically present while "he makes his answer."

Now this physical presence of the speaker differs from the purely mental presence of "this is an answer." I can vivisect any sentence from a book in the classroom and say that "it is." But I can be physically present only in a historically limited number of cases. My sentence "he is answering him" is much more specific about my own person than the other: "this is an answer." The pure brain is free to say the latter sentence. The whole man — legs, arms, rump and brain — must exist in the same place and time for the former. The speaker of the sentence "this is an answer" is an abstract being. The speaker of the sentence "he answers him" is a concrete being of flesh and blood who actually describes what he sees with his senses and interprets it only with his understanding.

Is this perhaps the contrast between speech and thought which we discover here? I think it is. All spoken language places speaker and listener in a definite, concrete relation to the truth. Thought, on the other hand, places us in an abstract, academic relation to it. The whole man speaks; the mind only reflects. When we close our eyes and reflect, we are free to leave parts of ourselves behind. When we open our mouth and ears to listen and speak, we are expected to gather ourselves up, from tip to toe. We may not do so. A thinker may think body and soul. A listener may not participate except with his mind. But the fact remains that in each case different expectations are aroused. Thinking blurs and tends to obliterate the relation of a sentence to the lifetime and the life-space of speaker and listener — or in our world, of paper and paperhangers, of writers and readers. In fact, the abstract sentence, we may venture to suggest, is conditioned by its literary character. Speech, in its origins, was unwilling and incapable of formulating sentences into which speaker and listener did not enter. This follows from the situation of oral speaking.

The reason why the Bible discounted statements like "this is an answer" may even have some connection with the purely paper character of such statements. This, however, is not for us to decide at this juncture. We are still in search of the origin of speech. And we may be satisfied to know that "this is an answer" is not a sentence from which to start. That does not detract from our real interest in sentences of this type. It is possible to discover the original place of these clauses in society. They are sentences of identification. They were invented in court for identifying "things." "Things" were objects of complaint of which the plaintiff said that they were his, while the defendant denied it. Things were "murder" and "theft" and "embezzlement," acts punishable by law which the plaintiff tried to introduce into the record. But the defendant cries: not murder but self-defense, not theft but a joyride, not embezzlement but a loan. Then the court identifies the act: It is manslaughter, it is petty larceny, it is embezzlement, says the verdict of the jury.

"This is" sentences are judicial sentences which make no sense unless they sum up contradictory proceedings. In every sentence such as "this is," we conclude a trial. "This is larceny" is true only after plaintiff and defendant have presented their opposing points of view. The term has been presented, has been denied, and now it is established. The plaintiff used the narrative: "He came into the room, fired a pistol and killed my father." The defendant used another narrative: "He forced me into the room and lifted his pistol; I wrestled with him and took the pistol from him; the shot went off in the process." The identifying verdict: "This is manslaughter," is a statement of fact very similar to 2 and 2 equals 4. It subsumes certain narratives into a logical relationship to a principle or precedent. But it is dependent on these narratives as its data of speech. "Ordinary" speech, complaint, defense and testimony must have preceded a verdict. Sentences of identification establish that which was not established before but merely claimed. Judicial verdicts create timeless truths because the times and places of the deeds have been told beforehand in the declamations of the parties.

The logic of any abstract sentence demands that it be preceded by specific and concrete data. No abstract sentence is true without such antecedents of concrete data.

This has tremendous consequences. Our judgments are based on data, not on facts. Data are things told; reality does not enter the court of our judgment mute, inarticulate and unformulated. Before we can make up our mind, reality has always already been told in various ways — it has been talked of by interested parties, in certain language, with certain words and verbs and sentences. Judgment is a secondary process in which the mind, regardless of person, judges things narrated, spoken, told, indicted and excused, claimed and defended. The very word "thing" should enlighten us.

Thing is the term for "court," (as *Ding* and *Sache* are in German), and later it is any object taken to court. Judgment is passed in court after the "thing" has been discussed, claimed and narrated by speaking humanity.

We cannot judge before we have been spoken to. Speech never appeals to pure reason. Whatever I say, I use names like America, Germany, Jews, Negroes and Japanese, which are full of dynamite. Nobody can tell a tale without exposing the listener to all the associations which accompany every single word. Some sound sacred, some ugly in his ear. Turn as he may — he will not get facts but narrative; never does a listener, a jury or a judge hear reality itself; they always hear people telling them about reality. And the reflecting mind is in no better position than the judge. Of course he will listen to pro and con; he will reflect on the arguments. But argument he must hear. And argument is speech loaded with associations of certain times of my life, of certain places in my existence. We understand the word America and New York in the very sense in which we have experienced facts about them. All data is historical and therefore told by somebody to somebody else. 2 plus 2 equals 4 is no exception. To believe that 2 plus 2 equals 4 we must believe that the specific qualities of the two pairs may, for the time being, be safely neglected. The whole truth of the argument in 2 plus 2 equals 4 depends on this. Theoretically Hitler and Stalin and Churchill and Roosevelt could be said to be four. But it makes little sense to apply arithmetic to those men. It does make sense to say Hitler, Mussolini, and Hirohito are three. It also may make sense to say that Churchill and Roosevelt are two statesmen. It also may make sense to compare or contrast Hitler and Stalin. But in politics 2 plus 2 equals 4 is nonsense. The logic of figures has its strict taboos.

The logic of the abstract statement is not as universal as we are made to believe. It depends strictly on a previous agreement in our argument that names don't matter. Mathematics is built on the negation of names. When named speech is not relevant, numerals may be introduced. Otherwise, they can't be. The logic of numerals is based on the denial of the existence of names. The functioning of numerals depends on the proof that names, in this case, are irrelevant. But in itself the logic of arithmetic is unable to vouchsafe its own application. Abstract statements remain ignorant of their own authentic place. This is true of all abstract statements. They make sense only in connection with and as the conclusions of real concrete statements which date the facts in relation to listener and speaker and which, for this reason, must use narrative speech and the concrete names of the people, the places and the times concerned. The logic of abstract statements and generalizations has an a priori: concrete utterances made in the light of great names.

It is, then, illogical to build a complete logic on the logic of abstract statements. The omission of other forms of speech in favor of abstract or mathematical expressions can only be made in every instance after the full drama of human dialogue has declared the names as void of meaning, in this particular case. Voiding must precede abstraction. Our gravedigger — the classifying, enumerating, abstracting faculty of the indicative — can do his work only when the thing to be classified has been voided of life. The logic of a living universe lies not in abstractions. Abstractions are in order for "things" and universes devoid of life. But speech was not established for such a purpose. Speech was established to call forth life.

This relation between speech and thought has a very serious consequence for thinking. A man cannot be called a thinker just because he can think "logically" in schoolhouse terms. For he must have participated in processes by which life is called forth. This is indispensable, since otherwise he does not know when "things" are dead enough to be subjected to abstract treatment. Today millions of people are told that they can "think" about the world and mankind and peace in general. But they are not told that nobody can think unless he knows from personal experience how to make a promise good, how to share a community's joys and sorrows, and how to tell the story of an event with respect and sympathy, as one who can identify with the event. No mathematical curves will help the psychologist or historian who constructs general laws unless he realizes that he must have shared in the lifegiving processes of speech before he can be entrusted with giving out those death warrants on former speech which are called generalizations.

### Speech As A Social Process

The supreme logic of the sentence "this is an answer" is not to be found within its own structure of the four words, "this," "is," "an" and "answer." The logic of the much belabored "Socrates is a man, all men are mortal, Socrates is mortal "doesn't lie inside the three articles of the syllogism. The highest logic of these sentences resides in their correspondence to experienced data of previous speech.

Theorists of modern science have nearly always eliminated their own experiences with speech. They have not admitted that their statements of abstract science are not related to facts in nature alone. These statements must correspond to what has been said in the high language of names in which the thinker participated and by which peace and order were called into being in society. To use the previous example: the man who says 2 plus 2 equals 4, may mean two apples and two pears, two army and two navy men, two girls and two boys, two allied and two axis statesmen. He must "know" men, apples and soldiers before he can be allowed to posit 2 plus 2 equals 4. This equation is an empty tool; and woe betide us when childish brains apply it in psychology or politics or history or art or education to four entities which shouldn't be added up. When Mohammed and Mary Baker Eddy and Jesus are lumped together as "three founders of religion," the inanity of so-called scientific or logical thought reaches a peak from which a disastrous downfall becomes inevitable.

The modern mind stultifies its own effort by not confessing the two opposite kinds of knowledge: knowledge which takes time and knowledge which takes no time. In our list of logical sentences: "answer me," "may I have an answer," "I have answered you," "he is answering you," the time element in each statement is unmistakable. "Answer me" precedes the act asked for; the run of time which my imperative set in motion will lapse when you can say "I have answered you," but not before. The imperative not only commands the listener; it at the same time lights up an alley of time into the future. A trail into time is beaten by the logic of any order given. A high tension current places the moments following the order under the expectation: will this command be followed up and fulfilled? The term "fulfillment" used in this connection is significant. By the imperative, time is formed into a cup, still empty but formed for the special purpose of being filled with the content demanded by the order. The action following the order is not a blind accident of the moment. By having been ordered, it has become organized into one "time span" which stretches from the moment in which the order was given to the moment in which the report is echoed back: "order fulfilled."

Orders connect two separated human beings into one time span, of which the imperative forms the expectation, the report the fulfillment. The secret logic of any imperative, then, lies in the peculiar tie between speaker and listener. The speaker makes himself dependent on the listener's response: he is fishing not for compliments but for someone to comply with his order. In this act he offers a fusion between the two biological times of two individuals. Everybody, as the doctors today say, has his own biological time within which his individual acts occur. On the eighth day of a wound received, let us say, the healing process of my body may proceed at one rate of speed, on the twelfth day at quite another. This biological time, then, is organized within or "under" my individual skin.

The logic of an imperative and its corresponding report demands that a supertime be established which neglects the separation of two bodies and their biological times. The order given by one person and the other's reporting back correspond so much to each other that they beget one common time. Everybody is talking today about "frames of reference." What we find between people who trust one another in commands given and fulfilled is not a frame of reference but a field of correspondence. The distinction is fundamental. A "frame" seems to exist outside our sayings or acts. This field of correspondence, however, comes into being by sayings and by acts, and does not exist outside of them. The field breaks down the separation of two "self-contained" bodies; it gets "under their skin," and they act as a single will from the moment the order is given to the moment it is reported fulfilled. After this, the field collapses and disappears. Its tension differs therein from a frame of reference which is purely abstract.

Now, the ancients when they spoke experienced exactly this temporary disappearance of their skin barriers, of their bodily separation. In innumerable symbolic acts, they expressed the experience that they formed one body with one skin. They went together under one hide, or they spoke of the body politic, or they drank each other's blood. Uppermost in their mind was the unity of speeches and acts which were parts of one and the same inspired movement running through two or more physically divided individuals.

We have difficulties in reconstruing the situation in which sentences were considered to be real acts and acts were considered elaborations of sentences. Our every-day language is too mercurial compared to high speech. When the President of the United States vetoes a law, and when a general gives an order, we still have clear cases of correspondence. In the first case, the order is not fulfilled. This brings a useful clarification. Vetoes are exceptions which explain the rule that the President usually does report back to Congress that the law will be executed by the Chief Executive and his staff as it was enacted. The formal veto helps to explain the often-overlooked fact that a law passed by Congress commands the Executive branch of the government to enforce the law. Laws not enforced are bad laws. The army, sheriffs, police, and government agencies are asked by Congress to carry out their orders; the veto is a report back: I won't. In contrast hereto, a general's order cannot be vetoed by his subordinates. And his order does not end until he hears that it is fulfilled. Here, then, are two clear, authentic cases for formal speech. And in both cases the logic of speech demands that the two sentences "march into Germany" and "we have marched into Germany" are understood as two pieces which do not make sense apart from one another!

This is a revolutionary statement. All grammar, all linguistics and all formal logic have held that sentences are the independent elements of speech. This cannot be admitted any longer. They are interlocking. Imperative and narrative are two aspects of one speech. Both have to be said before either makes sense or creates an epoch. The trouble with linguistic discussions has been that they always stopped at the analysis of the "completed" sentence. In so doing, the reason for grammar remains invisible. "March" and "we have marched" are not two different tools such as a hammer and a wrench I may have in my tool chest. "March" and "we have marched," correspond to each other as aspects of one process which forms a cup of time until it is fulfilled!

In our flabby speech, this is obscured because we do not assign to speech long avenues of time. While laws and army orders take weeks and months and years before they are reported as finished, an order given by a mother: "Take this sandwich," is answered by the child with words before anything is done. Johnny may say "Thank you," or he may say "Why?" or he may say "I don't want any," etc. We are so accustomed to such immediate answers that, when I asked my students for the proper answer to an order given, they all gave examples of this type.

A Hindu story may put us on the right track about the correspondence by which languages are created. (I owe it to Philip Wheelwright). A Hindu father says to his boy "my son, break the twig." The question then arises which is the correct answer for the son. The proper answer, said the Hindu sage, is: "my father, the twig is broken." Here, the family is still on a level with political group life. The father governs, the son carries out. "Break" and "broken" are aspects of one and the same act which lies between the two sentences spoken. The logic of these two sentences, then, is their place before and after an act willed by two people. These people change places after the act. One speaks in advance, the other speaks afterwards. He who speaks first listens afterwards; he who speaks afterwards listens first.

But in this case the logic of the situation is not "a dialogue," as we often are told. In a dialogue of Plato or Galilei people go on talking. In speech of high and authentic form considerable time elapses between the two fundamental sentences. It is not a dialogue when "march" and "we have marched" or the "oyez, oyez" at the opening of court and the ending formula interlock. It may be called a "drama" because the people speak and act, and act and speak.

Three features, we propose, distinguish speech in its authentic place from all texts analyzed by the tradition of linguistics. First, speaker and listener exchange places. The speaker becomes listener; the listener becomes speaker. Second, this changes the style of the sentences spoken. In advance, the imperative puts a burden on the listener. Afterwards the narrative unburdens this listener who reports back and quite literally carries back the burden put on him before the act. Third, sentences are the beginnings and endings of actual changes in the physical world. They are not "mental" or "intellectual." They are not thoughts communicated. They remove a barrier which physically divides two people, fuses them despite their bodily separation, and then closes this barrier again. These speeches are as much cosmic processes as the breaking of the twig. They proceed in the outer world as sound waves between mouth and ears.

The ancients never acknowledged that speech was not corporeal. To them it was as corporeal as the twig that moved through the air and connected two wills for a time span. Applying this to modern conditions, we should admit that a war does not begin when it becomes "a shooting war" and that it ends only when its history is reported in such a way that both parties will accept it as the report of this war. The words are part of one undivided social process; the processes which move forward through speech and act are social processes. And no process is social which is devoid of this opening and closing of human cooperation by authentic speech.

Formal speech is a physical process in the realm of our five senses by which a time cup is formed and dissolved. Within this time cup or time span or field of correspondence, human beings divide their labor. They cannot divide their labor unless they have entered into the common field of formal speech. And they cannot go on to new divisions of labor until the old field has been dissolved. Prior to all social acts the field of correspondence in which the acts are expected and fulfilled must be formed, and then that field must perish.

The forms of language move people who speak and who listen into the field of correspondence and out of it again. Speech is movement. The sound waves produced are not purely material or just tools. They themselves share the character of the relation because "break" and "broken," "march" and "we have marched," "answer" and "I have answered" are phonetically related to each other. We can recognize "broken" as related to break, answered to answer, march to marched. Without this correspondence speech would not have the form which moves men. "Break" is said because "broken" will be said. And "broken" makes sense because "break" preceded it. This differs from music and it differs from thought. In music, we repeat, although we may vary. In speech variation is constitutional, although we may repeat. A listener who repeats "break," "break," "break," ceases to be a doer; he becomes a chorus who repeats the burden or refrain. A speaker who says "broken," "broken" after the report may do so from consternation, but he has nothing to say himself!

Grammatical correspondence differs likewise from thought. In this case, we omit action and correspondence. To think means to condense command, act and report into one form. The scientist who muses over a new formula has accepted the commands: "There shall be science," "Be thou a scientist," and "Help science over its obstacle on this day." He deliberates and in this deliberation he has his action. And he reports in his formula. But it is an error to overlook the challenge and demand to which the thinker responds. The line is quite sharp which divides thinker and dreamer. A dreamer is not under orders to think. Hence, his results often are negligible. A thinker deserves this name only if he acts within a progressing column of thinkers in his place and time. The order which he hears asking him to solve this specific problem dates his effort as meaningful in the strategy of science. It is his marching order, just like any soldier's, though he articulates it only to himself. And without these data no atom smashing, no magnesium, no radar, no science is possible. These data are not of the thinker's own making. He receives it within a continuum of expectation and fulfillment which today we are accustomed to take for granted. But it has been built up and has daily to be rebuilt by people who acclaim this particular division of labor between science and society.

The vacuum created by modern theory for speech dishonors speech, thought and action equally. Speech is made a tool of thought. Both are contrasted with action. But no society knows of any social act without a division of labor as Marxians say, or without the Word as the Christians claim. Both are right, the godless and the godly. There is no social action which can be contrasted with speech. All acts are embedded in speech and the movement created by the first imperative "March into Germany," carries all the actions of millions of men until it can die down in the last platoon's report.

Taking sentences in their most pedestrian reality, we have classified them as sound waves. We have found that the sound wave "break" or "march" ultimately recoils upon the speaker's ear in the forms of "broken" and "marched" so that he now may dismiss himself from this field of interaction. Thus far, analysis of the two verbal forms showed that "broken" has an a posteriori aspect as compared to "break" as an a priori form. They seemed variations. This analysis did not go far enough. The relation between the imperatives: "oyez!," "go!," "act!," and their perfects: "We all have heard that which has been said at the hearing," "We have gone," "We have acted," etc. is not simply a variation.

### The Imperative

In more than fifty languages which I have analyzed for this purpose, the form of imperative sentences is the shortest, simplest, most unvaried and unencumbered form of the verb.[2] Everybody who knows Latin, German, Greek or Hebrew may test this fact easily for these languages. The earliest form of any verb has survived in these languages and has become the specific form for commands. I have stated the situation in the most cautious manner. I do not say that the imperative form in any of these languages originally was an imperative. But I do insist that the most original form of the verb became more and more restricted in its field of application and that, in the languages I have analyzed, it now serves the purpose of imperative sentences.

This is accepted by all linguists who have reflected on the history of the Indoeuropean verb — Waickernagel, Debrunner, Sommer, etc.[3] The situation in Chinese and in the Ugro-Finnic and Turko-Tatar languages is not different, but often the grammatical inflections for other aspects of the verb are not developed. In English most observers will find "go" to mean the infinitive ("to go"), the first person singular ("I go"), the second person plural ("you go"), just as much as the imperative by which a "thou" is asked to go. But on closer inspection they will find this to be a statement borrowed from their Latin grammar book. "Go" is the second person singular of the imperative and the shortest form of the verb, in English as in all other Indoeuropean languages. It is *not* the first person plural, the singular, the infinitive or anything else.

The infinitive reads "to go," the first person singular reads "I go." Neither "to" nor "I" can really be omitted. In the sentences "I make you go" and "You have seen me go" the "you" and "me" are necessary. This is borne out by the fact that, when the personal pronouns are missing, we prefer to say: "I observe going," "I hear the playing of the piano." The forms "I go," "you go," "we see him run," all need a special form for the person whose act the verb is said to express before we can recognize them as verbs; or they need a "to" or an "-ing" to disclose their character as action words. But the imperative is as rich as it is short. *"Fer," "tolle," "lege," "sta,"* in Latin denote a listener in whose trust a verb is placed, who is credited with future action, besides denoting the kind of action. Three different facts are expressed in the shortest form of any verb:

1. That somebody receives an invitation to act.
2. That the act lies in the future.
3. That the act is of a specific nature.

The imperative form of the verb preserves the most ancient layer of human speech. It may be called the vocative of the verb. For it invokes the original situation of formal speech in this original situation: a time cup is formed, two human bodies are temporarily fused into one will, a division of labor is initiated, a part of the external world is expected to change. Two people begin to move in the direction of this change. And the one word "fire!" sets all these processes in motion because it singles out 1. a human being who is asked to obey, 2. a worldly act which is required, 3. a time span which is set aside for obedience and for the act. All three achievements are formidable.

1. Obedience is a "psychological" attitude, or more correctly a social one. The listener is made into a soldier; when he learns to obey this command, he accepts a status in society. When a young girl rebelled in the family of my friends, she said, "You are treating me like a servant." The lady, who had an Italian butler, grew indignant: "How dare you say that! A servant is a skilled, trustworthy person who sustains the household by his eagerness to serve truly. I would never dream of bestowing on you the honorable name of a servant, for which office I have the highest regard. You are far beneath a servant. You have not even learned to obey." Imperatives transform people into participants in a social process. To provide 60 million jobs after the war is but a veiled expression for 60 million long-range imperatives which shall order people into social functions.

2. The specific word "fire" or "water" or "go" betrays the confidence of the speaker that he knows the world and what is wrong with it. The expert's confidence in his skill is in the mother's, the officer's or the fireman's order. Imperatives presuppose mastery of some subject in the universe. In the imperative knowledge is subordinate to responsibility. In the indicatives "this is an answer," or "this is the arm," the speaker is solely responsible for the truth of his statement. In imperatives he makes himself responsible not for stating a fact but for staging an act. The realm of his responsibility is not "science" or "thought" or "truth," but righteousness, history, and goodness. His sentence provides a cure for a deficiency of the real world, the cosmos as we find it, material, physical, chemical, biological and social. "Give the mad man a cold shower" is on the one hand an expression of knowledge about madness and its treatment, but over and above this confidence in knowledge, it assumes responsibility for restraining madness on the basis of knowledge. The intellectual aspect of an imperative sentence exists but it is subservient to the aspect of healing. Any imperative proves that the world cannot go on as it has been known to be. The little sentence "fire" or "march" decides that the man who speaks is fed up with mere knowledge of the world and goes over to a next phase by which the world is to be changed, on the basis of his understanding. The wealth of verbs from antiquity shows

the whole pride of professional language: toast, roast, broil, braise, cook, barbecue – what a wealth of verbs for the various ways of changing food! From the very beginning man's pride in speaking centers on the distinction of acts on the basis of skill and expert knowledge. But in authentic speech the verb is always the basis, never the crown, of speech. And the imperative ranks higher than the indicative in social relevance and logical perfection. It transforms known life into future lifegiving actions. The imperative, the most ancient sentence, trans-substantiates the world.

3. The imperative decides. This brings out the fact that it defines an epoch. Not a "thought" but a new order given marks the day as a particular day. Imperatives, not astronomers, make men move in history. Historical life is a sequence of imperatives. It is not the accumulation of knowledge or the evolution of science or the growth of machinery or the increase in speed which mark out the progress of mankind. It is the infinite sequence of commands given and obeyed which enlighten the times of history.

All this is to be found in one single imperative. The things of the world are mastered, times are decided, people are made by it. Light, outline, determination, flood the universe by the decision to give and to obey orders between two or more men. The light of reason never shines as brightly in any mere statement of fact as it shines in the right command given and obeyed at the right time!

### Between Order and Realization

Imperatives have made man feel enlightened, not indicatives. By ascribing light to the imperative, we have opened the path to an understanding of those sentences which express the great political imperatives of authentic speech. But what may we ascribe to the narrative if we exalt the imperative as the lightgiver? Why is "broken" less enlightening than "break!"? Is this not a foolish and haphazard remark? This would be true if the narrative "We have marched into Germany" were considered as less enlightening, less luminous than the order of Fortinbras at the end of *Hamlet*. But the sound waves of speech acquire a quality altogether lacking in the imperative. An imperative may wake us up, it may frighten us or clarify. But it is lacking the quality which the words of the Hindu boy, "My father, the twig is broken" possess. The narrative warms our heart. We say, "well done." The narrative is like the warmth of the fireplace in a home. It makes us feel good to hear the great deeds of the past well told and reported. We feel assured and protected by their narration.

Enlightenment is not the only purpose of history; it must be a light that warms our heart or it is not history but physics. Our fears while we listen to the tale are: will they obey their highest calling. If the tale ends in woe, it actually has not ended. It follows us into our dreams; it remains with us and we shall have to do something about it. Narratives with negative endings have not ended when they are told. The happy ending of Hollywood is required lest people can't sleep afterwards. It is legitimate to require an ending which sets a full stop. And the only full stop comes when that which was the thing to do from the beginning can be said to have been done in the end. Warmth in the end corresponds to light in the beginning. It was the error of the Enlightenment of the 18th century to deny this relation of light and warmth. They gave light the whole credit for organizing society. But the light of reason which does not come back to Prometheus in the form of a heart-warming report of human obedience would not be light. That everybody in our time can ask anybody else on the street for "a light," that is for "fire," is the great triumph of Prometheus.

The universal praise we give to that god who stole the fire lies in the fact that we have declared that everybody must give fire to everybody else. We have erased the term theft in connection with fire. In behaving like good communists with regard to fire we have followed Prometheus. Our usage should warm his heart. A survey would show his absolute victory, the total obedience of all men to his great command: "Let man have fire." And this was indeed Aeschylus' solution to the curse of Prometheus. When the Athenians built a temple in honor of Prometheus in which they gave him praise as "the firegiver," the painful abuse of the Titan ceased, and Zeus was reconciled by the praise and gratitude of men. The trilogy which begins with *Prometheus Bound* ends with a third play whose solution mystifies all rationalists. To him who understands history as a correspondence of imperatives and narratives, the redemption by heart-warming human gratitude will not appear anything but normal. The vulture's eating of Prometheus' liver stops. The wound heals.[4]

But what happens between "light" and "warmth?" How do sound waves ultimately produce warmth in the human brain when they begin as light?

"From brain to heart" must form a parallel to "from mouth to ear." The speaker sees his way clearly from the start; the listener rewards him by imparting warmth to his heart at the end. What happens in the meantime? Is the movement of social action during its execution without speech? Is speech the correspondence of imperative and narrative only? No, it is not.

The logic of sentences does not stop at beginnings and endings of social actions. During the action, too, sentences are in order, they vibrate like musical cadences in the nervous system of the people to whom the order was given. The commander "expects"; he looks out for the report. Therefore he is the prisoner of his own command. Prometheus suffers before his success is assured: before man renders him the only thanks which can redeem his lightning stroke of genius — to make fire universally available to every man and woman. Girls perhaps would not smoke so much if they did not enter, through the little match lit and passed on, the "Prometheus Club" which for thousands of years had been the exclusive right of men. Men lit fires; women preserved them.

Thousands of years may stretch between an order or promise and its realization. Indeed, all the great and important commandments already stand established today, and the only problem is are we going to do something about them? Let us look at an example. In 1910 William James wrote his *The Moral Equivalent of War*, a promise and prophecy, and a proposition to be acted upon. By 1940 nothing had been done about it. Everybody "knew" the essay, and everybody ignored it! This is an example of logicians' eternal ignorance of knowledge. Two great wars instead proved James's thesis that, without a moral equivalent, "war must have its way." This is a striking example of the slow start of new authentic speech in society. Here is the new term, the new condition of peace announced, and a curse is laid on inaction: "otherwise war must have its way." However, the speaker has found no listeners, just readers. James was a prophet and a saint, and he was treated simply as a writer of stimulating fiction. And wars had and have their way, more brutally now than ever before. In other words, when a new imperative is given and goes unheeded, the results are much worse than they were in the days before the new way into the future was proclaimed.

*The Lyric*

On this march into the future our courage, our interest, our hope must be kept brimming inside the time cup. Once an order is given, we need "morale" to go through with it. How is this done? We must be on fire. Enthusiasm is needed for success. And enthusiasm is lyrical. Soldiers sing when marching; any group on the way to and from work looks for some rhythm, for some rhyme to contain the reason for their action. We sing, we move on schedule as commuters, as smoothly as we can to carry out the order of the day.

Thus lyric is placed between dramatic and epic. It fills the time of expectancy: the goal is established but not reached. In our first examples, "May I have an answer!" was the sign of a pressed heart. "Let us sing while we wait or work away," would be the comparable expression for our lyrical situation. It has its own grammatical form, usually called the subjunctive. In Greek it is called the optative, in Latin conjunctive. It is, however, much more comprehensive. It is the mood of deprecation and curse, of blessing and praying, of rejoicing and wailing, of laughing and crying. To call it the lyrical mood would be logical.

This lyrical mood is relatively well established among modern thinkers thanks to Heinrich Maier's *The Psychology of Emotional Thinking.*[5] Maier, however, made it into "thinking," while it is actually lyrical speech. He gave it a monopoly for the whole realm of thinking which is not objective, that is which does not take the final form of "this is an answer." Maier and the teachers of English who teach poetry are usually neither soldiers nor lawyers nor priests nor historians. And so the world of speech has been divided between judgments and emotional sentences. The fountainhead of speech — the rational, decisive and incisive command — thereby remained buried. Commands are wholly unemotional and they are not judgments.

The preponderant interest of the literary man in poetry and fiction makes it necessary to contradict the dichotomy of speech into poetry and science. The result is that they distinguish speech as either rational or irrational, making any further research into the logic of speech impossible. It is worse to admit "irrational" speech than to overlook it completely. If all speech outside the gravedigger analysis, the statement of facts — "this is an answer,"

"Socrates is a man," — were "irrational" (and such dogmatic statements have appeared in print), the entire history of human forms of speech becomes inexplicable. Lyrics and poetry became separated from sacrament and report at the very late stage of the Homeric poems, as I have been able to prove in an essay on Homer. They existed previously but sailed in tow of their mightier sisters: "prayer" and "oath." The older layer cannot be derived from the younger. People have obeyed orders and have reported orders fulfilled even though the execution was not enhanced by lyrics. But the execution will lack in fulfillment unless the people in the process feel the spirit descend on them and are given a second wind, lyricism, to carry out their life's calling. To be on fire is a condition of a life really being fulfilled. This fire, however, should not be confused with the impure flame of our brutal passions. This fire must stem from the pure light of inspired reason evinced in the voice which directs any great and important decisions in life. Inspired enthusiasm leads to song, mere brute passion to vice.

Lyrics have their logical place and their grammatical forms between imperative and report, because they allow men to be on fire without becoming brutes. The 300 Spartans who died at Thermopylae, we may be sure, sang the great odes of Tyrtaios during the battle. This enabled them to be reported on in the famed distich:

"Stranger, go and bring the message to the Lacedaemonians

 That we are lying here in obedience to their laws."

The greatness of lyrics, of music, of dance and song, lies in the fact that it stems from reason instead of from physical urges alone. Poetry is not irrational at all. It is much more rational than mathematics. "Two and two is four" is a statement made by the brain in its gravedigger abstraction from the objects involved in the enumeration. On the other hand, "The wrath sing, goddess, of Peleus offspring Achilleus," evokes one of the most feverish passions which devour us. The lyrical mood descends into the dark depths of our body and carries the light of reason into the bottomless pit of the fires of sex, fear, jealousy, ambition, greed, and pride which are born in these depths. And the speech which articulates and objectifies these emotions is to be called irrational? Certainly not in any other sense than irrational figures in mathematics! The topics of song are men's toil, sweat, and tears; *nel mezzo del cammin di nostra vita*, in the middle of our path through life, the lyrical mood must sustain the soldier of life's call, lest between beginning and end he be without the light of reason. The sighs "May I have an answer," "oh that I were one of the gods," "hail!," "woe!," are rationalizations which allow the reluctant physical and individual human to carry the yoke of time on his shoulders. The authentic place for the lyrical mood is "for the duration," that is for the length of time during which a command spellbinds us and until it is resolved or we are absolved of it.

The grammatical form of the lyrical mood neatly expresses this fact. The lyrical mood is bound up with the first person plural as well as singular. The same lengthening of the sounds which we find in the lyrical or subjunctive (*fasse, croisse, vivat, pereat*, as opposed to *fait, croit, vivit, perit*), and which especially in Greek is highly developed, appears in the first person of the so-called indicative in Latin, German and Greek. It landed there from the lyrical mood. *Amo* is entirely frozen lyrical form taken over into the later indicative. Why? Obviously because in song we are subjective and speak in the first, lyrical, form. Commands, as we have seen, insist on the listener's acting. The report of the Lacedaemonians who died at Thermopylae, and any other historical report, needs a messenger who can speak of the dead. Lyrics describe how the movement started by an imperative fires the imagination and the emotions of the doer involved in obedience to that imperative. It is introspective because speakers of the lyrical mood are like coals burning in the fires. Here lies the authentic origin of a "first person" in speech. All commands are silent about the commander. He is like the dark cloud out of which the lightning of order strikes. Originally heroes are outside the communication of feelings. In Aeschylus' tragedies the real event is that for the first time the inner life of the hero behind this command becomes speakable. But this was 480 B.C.; thousands of years had intermingled grammatical categories and had produced poetry as the switchboard between formal and informal speech. Even in the Greek of Aeschylus, however, the first person singular of the prosaic judgment mood (the indicative) still was a form of the lyrical mood![6] The indicative borrowed it and never saw cause to develop a form of its own. Sometimes the same relation exists between the form used in the imperative and in the second person singular of the indicative, e.g. in Latin. The influence of the imperative form *fer* on this form (*fes*) has been pointed out by Latinists. The second person was borrowed by the indicative from the imperative as was the first from the lyrical.

This will help us sketch the real anatomy of authentic grammar which is different from the Alexandrian grammar lists in all our textbooks.

### The Narrative

But first let us look into the forms of the narrative mood. The narrative uses all possible means to mummify the imperative. The Greek word *nika* (to be victorious) was carried like a hero from the battle field of Marathon when the runner shouted his proud *nenikekamen* (we have been victorious), and fell dead to the ground. In all Indo-European languages, reduplication of the original form signified the narrative or perfect of a report. The imperative is incisive, sharp; sharpness is concise. The narrative is blunted, it is lengthy. The epical and the military style are familiar contrasts. New is only the fact that the grammatical cells of language bear the same marks of distinction. The forms of grammar *are* the original styles! In the tiny cells of articulated speech, bestride – bestridden, get – gotten, hide – hidden, write – written, the same differentiation is attempted which distinguishes the style of the ten commandments from the style of Thomas Mann's Joseph trilogy.

Augmentation for the narrative by a special vowel increased this difference, as for instance in Greek. The principle of break – broken, go – gone is general; only the means vary. Reduplication was not the only means of describing the epical mood of the narrative with its relaxed sense of having gained infinite time through fulfillment.

The second contribution of the epical mood or narrative is its insistence on the third person plural: "the men fought well, but I alone escaped to tell you," or "this man was stricken down in an act beyond the call of duty" require distinct forms for the "third" person. The third person is a third person in one sense only; he is neither the speaking reporter nor the listening commander. But he is not a third person in the sense in which our grammars use the term. The third persons in the narrative, "he went," "they fell," were certainly created for real people, not for dead things. These people had spoken with, lived with, and belonged to the speaker and the listener! They were former speakers, singers, listeners and had participated in the common life. The third person is not purely numerical, but historical. *Fuerunt* means there have been men like ourselves before us. Identification is not precluded by the existence of a third person in grammar. Because time is of the essence in formal speech, the time cup includes those of whom the report speaks as having passed away. It is quite important to clarify the place of the third person in grammar. Our logicians treat it as their domain for abstract statements. We already have pointed out the borderline which divides a sentence like "they have answered you" from "this is an answer," or "2 plus 2 equals 4." They seem alike because both are formally in the third person. But worlds separate them. "They have answered you" is a complete, epical sentence. "2 plus 2 equals 4" is an incomplete abstract judgment.

## The Abstract

The character of sentences of judgment is elliptic at the cost of being incomplete. They are incomplete despite their alleged rational or reasonable character. The logic of the schools takes advantage of the elliptic quality to simplify truth to a lollypop of truth. No truth of relevance can be expressed in logic's elliptic statements because they omit decisive features: relations to persons and times are eliminated. Logical statements did not originally need these features because they were spoken in court. The judge and the jury say "guilty," in summing up the proceedings of a lengthy trial after days and days. "He is guilty" is a judgment which can forego any relation to the time in which he became guilty. "This is murder" is a judgment which omits the person, too. It is the logical operation of identifying an act and a law by subsumption. Hence the act is stripped of the agent and the actuality, person and grammatical tense, and becomes a verbal noun "the murder." But this fact is the result of speeches in which these tenses and agents were named, and it therefore is justified to speak of it as a shorthand statement.

Judgments are the first abbreviations. When they were taken out of court and handled in schools, we got "logic." All Greek philosophy imitates legal proceedings in its rooms. It is *polis* thinking outside the *polis*. Socrates induced Plato to transfer the mental processes of the citizenry of Athens from their social environment into the academy. On this strange path the last shorthand development of formal speech, the sentences of judgments, such as "this is murder," have become the basis of all discussions concerning logic since the fourth century before Christ. One might say that the logic of this logic overturns the sequence of the true process of grammatical language. It begins at the end of the process. The concrete speech which later allows us to become abstract, sentences which are complete with regard to person, act and time, imperative, lyrical mood, narrative are declared to be "irrational," and the abstract judgment which subsumes a pleaded case under some former statement of statute is declared to be the normal sentence in which reason finds its logical expression. The logic of the other sentence is not a bit less reasonable or logical. And, in addition, it achieves more, is richer in content, longer in life, more certain in time.

The abbreviated "this case is murder" allows us to shelve the case. This is its merit. We must get out from any one "correspondence" of sentences. The act of the actuarian performs an important service. It frees our memory from all the proceedings and from the temporal, personal elements of the sentences which preceded the judgment. It is abstracted from them, but how can anybody expect that the proceedings, the sentences spoken by real people about real things at a real meeting of their political group, in the courthouse or meeting house or on the commons, can be explained or derived or understood by the actuarian's remark: "O.K., shelved." This is what our logicians do all the time. They sit in judgment over language's performance and the first paragraph of books on logic is usually devoted to some complaint about the imperfections of language. With sovereign contempt they look down on language as rudimentary, archaic; and thought is exalted as the only rational process.

At this point, we shall not go further into the tragedy of occidental logic and its stubborn forgetfulness of the obvious.[7] The reader, will I hope, understand that the logic of the sentences of language is based on responses between people. For their exchange of sentences we had to avoid the term dialogue because, in the usual dialogue of today or of Plato, the correspondence is already emptied of the action which was called forth by the command, accompanied lyrically, and reported in the narrative. Dialogue does not extend over the generation, the decade or the year which it takes for the "promissory notes" of original language, the imperatives, to be cashed.

The term "correspondence" may also be misconstrued. But it is perhaps easier to give the original meaning of formal speech: to form a time cup of expectation and fulfillment between real people over long periods of time, for the great occasions of death and birth, festivals and holidays, initiation and marriage. Well do I know that a powerful objection may be raised to our whole vision: did people not converse on the spot? Do you really imagine that there was no dialogue in the modern sense from the very start? How can you prove such stilted and artificial handling of language by speakers or listeners? Is speech not always much lighter, easiergoing, and serving the moment?

This natural objection shall be answered in the next section. But it is necessary to keep it apart from the furor of the logicians who begin with a sentence of judgment against all the grammatical and linguistic evidence of five thousand years of monuments and who condemn the logic of pre-juridicial or prephilosophical speech from an academic chair which stands in a purely Alexandrian tradition and schoolhouse. The refutation of this pseudologic, it would seem to me, has been achieved by our positive insight into the cadence and respondence character of our grammatical forms, and by our re-establishing the field of force by which speakers, listeners and acts are moved through a common time span from the imperative's beginning to the story's end.

For the actuarian's act of storing spoken processes, I have more respect than this criticism of Alexandrian logic may seem to imply. One more word on its logic seems to be in order. In one way, it is elliptic because the drama between commander and obeyer is shelved. But in another way, the pure judgment acquires one quality lacking to the act in the logic of other sentences. This additional quality is its numerability! A judgment can treat this answer as one answer, that is as one answer among many. In the abstract sentence "plurality" enters the scene. That this is a net gain may be seen in the exclusive character of an imperative. "Give," "go," "harken" are of such selective power that any imperative deals with a unique situation. Unique decisions do make history because they are unmistakable as this unrepeatable "once for every man and nation" in which they make unrepeatable decisions. On the other hand, the subjective mood of a marching song, love song, work song or sailor's song is equally remote from a numerical estimate of the singers' emotions.

Narration, too, deals with the singularity of events. (A whole philosophy of history was based on this one true fact by some neo-Kantians.) But the actuarian deals with recurrence of events: first, second, and third Carthaginian war; first, second, seventh, and ninth spring festival. Any order which recurs must be able to shelve one period and to put another in its place. Time is rhythmical or is made rhythmical by the sentence which subsumes it. Long before the city of Athens had juries and courts, the primeval tribes held festivals, dances and rites at the full or the new moon, or on similar occasions. The numbering of these recurrences led to statements of judgment. In solemn ways the year was declared closed, or the cycle of holidays was opened with the great sentence: a new cycle begins.

A good example of the need of ritual for numbers is the following which necessitates counting up to 70. The Osage Indians require from the man who performs the rites of Wawatho or *Xó-ka* that he shall know all the sets of songs used in the ceremony, as a token of reverence to the ritual and of respect to the person whom these rites initiate. Two devices help him in this arduous task; one is a flat stick, one foot long; the other a bundle of rods. Lines are cut, on the flat stick singly or in groups, according to the number of songs in each set since each line represents one song and the number of songs varies from set to set. The bundle of sticks, pencil-width but one foot long are used during the ceremony and to instruct the new candidates. The sticks in the bundle number about 70. Both devices, it deserves to be noted, have the same name: "rods placed upon."[8]

In a way, these statements on numbers were as full of time sense as all other sentences. The dimension added to time was solely a repetition of whole times. First command, second command, third command – but all had their full development inside of which each one was treated as unique and incomparable. But when looked at as timespans, as episodes, they became comparable.

Counting by gesticulation, fingers and feet, etc. must be left aside here. Formal speech about three and thousand, four and fifty did not spring from our share in animal language. "Three" and "two" and "four" and "eight" were high words for big things, and their numbers were discovered and stated as solemnly as all other sentences. Our numerals made lived sentences comparable and stored whole cycles or correspondences of such sentences in an orderly fashion. "The one and the many" never obtruded itself as a logical problem. The one begins as "once," and it ends when it is classified as one of many. When the power to decide vanishes, as it had vanished in France before her fall, we may be sure that some pseudologic has tried to push "once" out of its place and to place "the many" in power at too early a moment of life. Jacksonian democracy was saved by American opportunity. For singular, unique opportunity came first in the days of youthful America. And opportunity was unique, now or never, imperatival, lyrical, a tall-tale. Democracy in the end was the summary of all these unique acts of pioneers. What are 48 states or 140 million Americans to a man who does not know what one American or what Rhode Island is able to do single-handed? 400 million coolies were no world power; 40 million Americans were!

The fallacy of logic when it tackles the eternal question of the relation between the one and the many lies in the neglect of the time element. Numerals come at the end; they express our faith in the recurrence not of single acts but in the recurrence of whole life cycles. When I say ten men, I speak in fact of ten biographies, of ten life times. If I say ten summers, I mean ten cycles crowned by summers. The dignity of our numerals is in their power to compare processes and lives. My fingers suffice to count apples. But to say: "the second act begins" one must do more than live in this moment. One must look into the past and into the future. And this was a solemn act in itself. To sum up also takes time.

He who says "this is an answer," transcends the was, is, and shall be of the three moods of speech by creating a sum of what is, what shall be, and what has been. The three are explicitly recognized as one and the same act. The Greeks were so impressed with judgments of this sort that they used the famous *aoristus gnomicus* for such statements and proverbs. The act of recognition that things would be again as they had been before and were now is a solemn act; it always expressed the discovery of a truth which goes beneath the surface of things. When the Greek said in the gnomic aorist: *Gnothi sauton*, the awe of "eternally so" went into this very special form. Such sentences were final. They were not spoken in the midst of acts of life. They were the end-results of living and were valid for all times and seasons.

It is true, however, that the time aspect of mathematics is implicit; it is the operations themselves which take time, since the mind abstracts numbers from recurrences. The form which time assumes in mathematical thought is mental time: it is not inherent in external things which are already named, have come into existence, and now "wait." For this reason they are abstracts. Time has been abstracted from them. An object is an act minus its time-element. Such an object offers no resistance to being shelved, numbered or classified. It is not their own time-aspect which colours the numerals used to speak of objects; but the fact that mathematics take time is a fact nevertheless. I know that logicians will consider this blasphemy. "Pure thought," they protest, "is timeless." To me, to whom our minds are as much a part of the created world as our bodies, their violent protest is perfectly understandable: abstraction is their only way of thinking. Despite their protests, it would seem indubitable to me that the sentence "all men are mortal" presupposes an operation of the mind which it has taken time to carry out. No statement about "all" can be made otherwise. All summaries, any remark about "all" presupposes a going over many individual statements at one time. "All" is an imperative of our curiosity. When we say "all" we have satisfied this curiosity and have "tamed" one domain of reality. It is a mighty presumption to say "all," so mighty that modern physics now deprecates "all" such statements.

The essential feature for us here is that the logic of numbers presupposes equanimity of the mind itself. During a mathematical operation one cannot change one's mind. The 400 years of modern mathematics since Cardanus are based on the belief in one and the same mind for all mathematicians. As laymen, as fathers or husbands, Euler or Bertrand Russell may change their minds; as mathematicians, who collaborate on numbers, they all must remain static and of one mind. The whole blight of the offices in which we are judges is in this inflexibility of any official mentality. The equanimity of mind in past, present and future distinguishes the judge in any field from the partisans, the leaders and followers in their animation.

This continuity of mind for judgment had to be discussed to prepare an answer to the question: what is the temperature of a mathematical statement? Light, fire, warmth are the qualities of speech which makes history; coldness is the temperature of speech which numbers and shelves history. The scientific sentence is detached, and therefore its speaker and his public must be indifferent to the heat engendered inside the processes which they classify and register. There is a definite change in temperature from the Declaration of Independence to the strange book title of 1933: *The Public and Its Government.* That is, indeed, an ultimate title for a book and an ultimate state of society. The public can't have a government, properly speaking. The Declaration of Independence might rightly be termed "The People and Their Government." People can be on fire, enlightened, elated.

The public, by its very nature, is an onlooker. It wants to be shown; it may be motivated by curiosity, spectacular impressions, sentimentality, perhaps, but all these are secondary and second rate influences. The people are called into being by being John Smith, American, private first class, husband of Anne Elizabeth Potter Smith, father of three children, etc.

It is a good argument in our favor that the verb *esse*, to be, of which "is" is a remnant in English, has no dramatic or imperative form. There is no real commanding form of "he is," since "be" is derived from another root. It would have to be "i" or something similar. But the whole group of *esse* — "essential," "essence," "being" — is abstract. People never are; they act and suffer and speak. When we say of anybody "he is a pedant," "he is a poet," "he is a Roman Catholic," we nearly always say too much and pigeonhole him. Nobody can be classified without injustice. It is wholesome American usage to say: he is Polish, he is Jewish, he is Irish, while the Europeans murder each other because they declare that "he is a Pole," "he is a Jew," "he is an Irishman," "he is an Italian." These titles in Europe have divided the nations so deeply that nothing common was left. Human life is dynamic. God has been called "pure act," *actus purissimus*. Gods and men never "are." The Gods speak: "Go," "harken," "come"; men sing: "we are going." But the very thing in which philosophy and logic delight, the study of being, is an abstract study, and the fact that it is an abstract study stands revealed in the little fact that "he is" has no imperative which goes with it! In every language there are some imperatives which do not proceed into further verb forms, like woe! heigh!, hello!, and also some narratives which have no imperative. The lacunae of grammar are instructive.

"The public" is a word abstracted from the adjective public which comes from *populus*, people. "People" itself belongs with the attitudes of drama, lyrics, epics, not with the abstract logical phase. Now we admire the abstract phase of speech as we admire the others. The cold temperature of the logical phase is necessary if our life is to be emancipated from "entangling alliances"; it helps us detach ourselves from our citizenship when we call America a modern "civilization." For the purpose of detachment, people became more "public"; the citizens of Athens who listened to the trial of Socrates became spectators. Socrates became "a sight" to them, and his friends gave up political action and became the "theorists," the "reviewers" of philosophy.

## The Full Cycle of Speech

The way speech proceeds from warm to cold transforms both speaker and listener in their relation to the speech act. The high-degree speaker is the Commander-in-chief, the leader; and his listeners are his people, his followers. The low-degree speaker is the mathematician; and his listeners are his public, his readers. In the first case speech begets action and is meant to produce action; in the second case speech is meant to induce inaction. We stand at attention when the flag is hoisted. The flag is the symbol of commanding speech. We sit down on our fannies when class begins. The classroom is the symbol of academic speech. Chieftain, cantor, historian, mathematician — are the diminishing degrees of speaking authority. Followers, fellows, listeners, public — are the diminishing degrees of hearing capacity. A chieftain has power over his fellows. A mathematician has power over his figures and circles. The chieftain attached men to himself. The mathematician has detached himself from all human association.

The cycle should now be transparent. The logic of sentences which *correspond* to each other binds and dissolves fellowships. The individual participates in society by passing all the time through these stages of leading or being led, of being moved or of remaining unmoved. Each time he is a different kind of person; the grammatical and the personal change carries us through states of *thou, I, us, and it* since we obey imperatives as *thous*, are moved by ups and downs as *I's*, remember *our* past and detach ourselves from *it*.

No human being stays in any one of these grammatical positions all the time. On the other hand, he is not a human being who is limited to any one of them. Slaves are always receiving orders. Hysterical neurotics are always emotional and subjective. Dead souls are always looking backwards into the glorious past, and clever profiteers are exclusively interested in figures. But man must expose himself incessantly to the transsubstantiation of his sound waves from light to fire to warmth to coolness.

A comparison between the usual grammar of our Alexandrian tradition as exposed by Heinrich Maier and the order discovered here may be apt to clarify the change in approach. Both grammatical lists have their usefulness. However, the catastrophe of occidental logic came when, as Maier put it, the very existence of a logic which was not the logic of judgments was forgotten and denied.⁹ And this catastrophe is expressed in our textbook grammars by the crude six-part tables of: I love, thou lovest, he loves; we love, you love, they love, etc. In these tables all persons and all times are ascribed to all aspects of speech. Real languages, fortunately, balk at this enterprise. A first person — "Hello, I say to myself: Go!" — does not exist in the genuine imperative, to the obvious disappointment of the author of my old Latin grammar. Imperative and second person "belong" to each other. But does the second person exist in the narrative? *Amavisti* (you have loved, s.) and *amavistis* (you have loved, pl.) are late crutches in Latin to supply forms which would round off the precise and specific *amaverunt* (they have loved), etc. This perfect is one of the strong forces of the verb, but it "belongs" with the third person *he* and *they*. Each mood has its person which it favors and which, originally, gave it its special quality. Our textbooks say that we may say:

| *amo* | *amem* | *ama* | *amabam* | *amavi* | *amare* |
|-------|--------|-------|----------|---------|---------|
| I love | O that I loved | love! | I was loving | I have loved | to love |

That is true, but it is a late and inappropriate treatment.

We protest that grammar becomes truly appropriate when we link one person with one mood as follows:

| dramatic (imperative) | lyrical (subjunctive) | epical (narrative) | logical (classifying) |
|-----------------------|-----------------------|--------------------|-----------------------|
| *ama* | *amemus* | *amaverunt* | *amor, amare* |
| *fide* | *confidamus* | *confisi sunt* | *fides, fidere* |
| be | that were | they have been | to be, being |
| *va* | *andiamo* | *andavano* | *andare* |
| *geb* | *(wie gern) ginge ich* | *sie sind gegangen* | *geben* |
| *i* | *iomen* | *eileluthasin* | *ienai* |

This list opens up the present state of society. To approach it, the reader should look at the imperatives once more. Especially expressive is the swelling up of the Greek for "go" (last example) to colossal pomp in the narrative or perfect from a short hiss in the imperative. The future presses upon us; the past gives up infinite time. This is not a poetical metaphor, but a true description of human time-relations. When we divide time into future, past and present, we moderns often commit the mistake of treating these three aspects of time as time units of an objective character. Nothing is less true. It is one of the most serious consequences of our surrender to Alexandrian logic that "time" is considered an "object." Time is an "aspect." The present simply does not exist except inside the time cup formed by imperatives.

When we, for instance, speak of the "present" state of science, our statement is meaningless for those who do not believe in science. They will deny that there is anything but 34 different Ph.D.'s all saying something different on the same subject. Only those who believe that there *must* be science can possibly find a real thread in all this confusion. They will produce the future of science by helping its progress through their belief. In the light of this future in which they believe, and in no other light, may they speak of the "present" state of science. To others who see the corruption, the vanity, the fashions — in psychology for instance — the chaos of our days may appear to be so incoherent that "a present state of science" seems to him a purely conventional phrase to cover the laziness and ignorance of some of its practitioners.

The "present" is an aspect of time which is invisible without our sympathy, without our opening up to the fulfillment of the specific command under which a present becomes visible.

A person who says that the present state of affairs is pretty satisfactory or that it is pretty bad admits his entanglement in it. He has mixed feelings about it. The lyrical mood is the mood of oscillations, vacillations — of *"himmelhochjauchzend zu Tode betrübt"* — of inertia mixed with somersaults. The lyrical mood of the emotional is unresolved, yet under the pressure of a definite imperative directing time to its appointed end. The reader should take note that this emotional state is a state of mind and completely rational when seen in its true time aspect.

Mixed feelings mark our participation in the present, and they are not irrational since they are founded on the in-between situation between the beginning and the end of one historical event. And it shows an open mind to keep the bad or the happy ending in mind. The same logicians who recommend the open mind as rational, and who call the lyrical mood irrational, overlook the fact that nobody has a more open mind than he whom doubt and fear and tiredness and hope toss up and down in his feelings. The really open mind is owned by the most irritable poet who gives in to every suggestion and stimulus of the split second and who is highly emotional. The imperatives and the narratives of life require acute and loyal minds. Lyrics flutter into every niche of thought because the issue is pitched but undecided.

The lyrical mood is the subjectivism of us moderns. This grammatical mood is inflated today. Nearly all of our intellectuals, all our liberals, are skeptics, doubters, emotionalists, subjectivists or lyricists under the pretense of having an open mind or of being rational.

The party of the future among us are the Revolutionaries, the communists and fascists, the Fortinbras who say: act first, think later. They are in a hurry. And indeed all future comes like lightning. The gospels are full of this truth. But in isolation the future is cruel for that very reason. Revolutionaries always treat time and all its suffering as negligible. In the name of the future, they build concentration camps, they let millions of people die in slave labor. When these victims are mentioned to the Party men, they shrug their shoulders: in the name of the glorious future, it had to be done. Any Revolutionary Party makes past and present victims of the future. The only aspect of time which they allow to speak is the future.

Our third party are the Evolutionists. Their principle seems to me just as extreme as that of our lightning Revolutionaries. They enjoy the past so much that every million years they can add to the history of life seems a net gain to them. We are told of 400,000,000 light years, of hundreds of thousands of years of man on this earth. These symbols of evolutionary thinking are not findings of science but prejudices of a definite aspect of time. When I remove myself and my mental processes lock, stock and barrel into one definite aspect of time, this aspect is all I can see or think or feel. The Evolutionists among us deliberately believe in the past and it is the logic of their own sentences which leads to their "endlessnesses" of time. When I narrate, I lengthen. When I treat reality as a story, it grows to infinity; when I treat it as an order of the day, it shrinks to a split second. When I waver, I suffer from torn-to-pieces-hood. Our three great parties of Revolution, Evolution, and Scepticism represent the three great aspects of grammatical time as follows:

| Revolution | Evolution | Scepticism |
|------------|-----------|------------|
| imperative | narrative | lyrical |
| future | past | present |

Each party is linked to a single aspect of articulated time. And each is separated from the healthy flow of speech through all three aspects of time.

Man's predicament is eternal. He has to form those various aspects into one cycle. They are our seasons. Man has no mastery over time without timing these seasons. They do not happen automatically. The three great parties of the modern mind are dogmatically enshrined, each in just one season of formal speech; therefore they have abandoned their liberty of timing, their actions, feelings or traditions in the proper rhythms of an articulated human society. The latter seems to be kept together by the struggle between the three parties. If all three are equally strong, we may get the benefit of their balance in the form of a cycle fulfilled; we also may get a vacuum in which all the seasons of the mind sterilize each other. The vision of the three great parties is not arbitrary in our investigation. We are writing the cellular pathology of language. Every word or sentence, to us, reflects precisely the same order as the whole social body. Every sentence is a cell out of the millions of cells which build up the conscious and formed life of civilization. The short sentence "the twig is broken" and Bancroft's *History of the United States* are of the same character to him who knows that "sameness" must express itself in different forms at different times.

One might group our experience of the grammatical forms as follows:

| *Narrative* | *Imperative* | *Lyric* | *Judgment* |
|---|---|---|---|
| tradition, truth | ethics, goodness | esthetics | science |
| loyalty | movements | beauty | system |
| history | politics | poetry | objectivism |
| literature | revolution | subjectivism | mathematics |
| evolution | | scepticism | |

This list is deliberately incomplete. In a German publication over twenty years ago I undertook a more systematic comparison between law, art, science and liturgy through their grammatical sentences. Until we realize that such tremendous modern phenomena as art and science are rooted in necessities of human articulation, no complete list of their slow unfolding from the simple sentence to the modern giants of civilization will be of interest. Once this sameness of structure in the cell and the whole body politic is understood, work on this can be undertaken by many in collaboration. At this point the sketch above may once more remind the reader of our peculiar method. We looked for the eternal origin of speech in our own midst, and this suddenly explained to us the purpose and structure of all formal speech. War was relieved by peace, revolution by articulation, anarchy by credit. Now we have simply repeated this form of proceeding. Since all human life is human insofar as it is lived in the light of commands, modern life is also to be lived in the same grammatical aspects of light, fire, warmth, coldness which were the states of man's consciousness ever since he spoke, was spoken to and spoken of.

## 7. Dress and Speech

I have assumed that men spoke formally over long periods of time. Is this not quite unbelievable? The time has now come to face this most serious objection. To the modern mind it is unbelievable. The ancients, on the other hand, believed that the whole of history was one short dialogue between creative and redeeming speakers. I was taken aback when I discovered that Martin Luther in 1517 literally responded to statements made by the Pope in 1202. Jesus was called the second Adam because he responded to God's imperative, but in the opposite manner from Adam. The respondences of whole nations to each other and the philosophical dialectics involved intrigued Hegel and Marx. But generally such beliefs are not well received among us. If the origin of speech as a series of respondences is to have any credibility, we shall have to support our thesis by other evidence.

This evidence is available. Our forefathers found ways and means to speak for an hour or a day and yet aim at a lifetime. Formal speech opened timespans into the past and into the future from one year to one hundred years. Yet the sentences which knitted together these corresponding points of time as promise and fulfillment were spoken and exchanged in much shorter periods of times.

We are helped in our argument by the one form of expression which is as universal in mankind as speech, by dress.

Dress expresses a temporary social role. A dress may be looked at as a uniform, a costume, a mask, a role. It has some of all of these qualities. No human group is without dress.[10] And this dress expresses a new state or condition. Dress not only covers, it also replaces the body.[11]

Let me quote from Elinberg's *Social Psychology:* "An English painter while traveling through New Zealand made a number of portraits of the natives, including one of an old chieftain whose face was covered with the spiral tattooing typical of his rank. The artist showed the model his picture, expecting his hearty approval. The old man looked at the portrait, then declined it with the words, 'That's not what I am.' The artist then asked the chief to draw his own portrait. When he handed the white man the result, with the words, 'That's what I am,' the latter could see nothing but the old chief's tattoo pattern, which signified his tribal connection."[12]

It is no use to smile at the chief's illusion. For it is not his illusion but the constitution of his clan which alone makes it possible to be and to act the chief. Nobody is deceived; nobody has any illusions. He has acquired a form of existence not existing in physical nature yet wholly real.

We have seen before that nobody can become the father of a family until somebody tells him he is and gives him the insignia of a married man.[13] A wedding must be enacted by a ritual on an extraordinary occasion in order to activate a marriage. The peace of the home depends on the festivals of the tribes, we said. And festivals of the tribe leave behind, as permanent tokens, some dress. The rules of life are based on exceptional events, its times created by high moments.

Strange ideas crop up where this is overlooked. In writing on the Zunis, Arthur Kroeber, one of our most distinguished anthropologists, admitted that the facts pointed to the fundamental role of their clans.[14] "But," he shouted angrily, "I shall not accept this." It would mean that the clan with its promiscuity, immoral origies, etc., preceded the family. Kroeber and his whole school overlook the place of speech and dress. Of course, we are not faced by an alternative between unregulated clan life and regulated family life, but the "irregular" holiday life gives names and dress and rules to daily family life. The clan brings the family into existence because it gives names and dress to husbands and wives. The facts about the primary character of the clans, and Kroeber's defense of the original role of the family are perfectly compatible. Dress expresses the temporary roles assigned to us by speech. And as often as we change to another "habit" or costume, so often do we change our social role, our body.

Dress has made men changeable. In every generation our physical organism must re-organize into new social forms. The very helplessness of our bodies commands us to establish through original adornments new groups in a perpetual stream called history. History is the constant making and unmaking of temporary social orders, territorial peaces, systems of credit, and articulated languages and literatures. Dress gives men the freedom to complete their physical nature by social organ-ship at a given time and in a given place. Dress is assumed and laid off again. We acquire, as I quoted before, a different body by putting on a doctor's gown, a priest's garment, a bathing suit or a nurse's uniform.

From the beginning, this "many-bodiness" is the real secret of men. Primeval man felt that he must "don" the eagle's feathers, the lion's mane and the elephant's proboscis, and thereby temporarily play their roles in society.

A piece of cloth may of course warm me, or may protect me against attack. Dress, however, is not simply a piece of cloth. Naked Indians will wear a loin cloth, and tattoo their bodies because social costume, not selfish utility, is their purpose in dressing. Dress gives one a station in the life of society. Most discussions stop at this point and then the relationship of dress and speech remains obscure. But closer inspection reveals a more complex purpose of dress. The complexity results from the fact that somebody who wears the eagle's feathers in a group is not only himself affected but also affects onlookers. It arouses in them the expectation: here is an eagle. And their expectation constitutes his power to act the eagle indeed! The triangular relation between bearer, onlookers and dress has to be analyzed.

Investiture with a social role gives power. The chieftain is free to act the chieftain as the nurse is free to nurse on account of their uniform. Men acquire freedom and power by investiture. The man whose head is garnished with feathers is promised a free hand by his followers. Any garment or robe bestowed upon a person opens an avenue of free action inside the social field defined by that dress. Forms of dress enable us to fulfill social functions in freedom and power. A dress is in the realm of time what a deed is for property in the realm of space. It is a legal title to a long road through time.

Dresses which we now change frequently were originally given for a lifetime. This lifetime usually began at initiation. So it was not a physical but a political and mental lifetime. But in these dressing ceremonies, primeval men showed the intent and ability to create organs of society, to organize groups over long periods of time. The dresses and tattoos of the savages bear out our contention that in human actions all men aim first of all at the great periods of life which connect whole generations. A dress did not serve for a few minutes in a night club but for the offices of society which lasted for a lifetime. The coronation ceremony of a British King is the best remnant of original investiture and formal speech among Western man. Here investiture and formal speech are of the essence.

Now, dress can give us the key to the problem of the time-span for speech. The coronation ceremony is ceremony; it is holiday-act. It condenses the mission of a lifetime into a few hours. The symbols of a coronation in one short day cover the whole realm of royal experience in peace as well as war. He is crowned as lawgiver, good regent, commander, Great Admiral, Emperor of India, Defender of the Faith. He is "celebrated." And to celebrate means to cumulate and to condense in one short moment the events of long periods of time.

In a coronation the grammar of life's correspondences can be made present. At first all speech was ceremony to condense into a short time-span an action which expressed the significance of a lifetime.

Will the reader kindly place the innumerable chats, songs and talks which he has had in his life so far, on one side of a mental ledger, and place on the other his own names, family and given, and all they have done for him or against him during the same period? If he does so conscientiously, he may recover this buried tradition of the human race: the ceremonies in which names were imparted. Your name, dear reader, gave you a background with innumerable people who knew your parents and your group before you existed. It classified you in some way or other unconsciously in the minds of those who knew you by name only. With other people, you yourself have given your name significance by your record. You have left your background as described by your family name and have inscribed your own name in the book of life. But in both directions, the names were there before you knew of them and regardless of what you thought of them yourself. Names create associations because they affect their carrier as well as the public.

We are told by psychology that associations are unreasonable and illogical. The whole school which pursues the study of associations scolds them as immature. On account of our broader logic, which includes the logic of action as well as that of science, we are no longer able to sneer at association as "mere" association. When I hear somebody mention one Eugen or Rosenstock or Huessy, I am interested. And this is the purpose of names. They intend to associate its carrier with other people. Names group. What is wrong with such a purpose? I may be associated with my background, my family, my playmates, or instead I may associate with my chosen associates of my later life. But associated I must be. The protest against pseudoassociations does not invalidate valid associations.

The condescension about the purely associative character of speech during the last century is easily explained. Wundt, Grimm, Bopp, Durkheim and Humboldt never completely separated names from words. Dictionary and grammar cultivated the fiction that we speak only by words. Thus the dictionary, that cemetery of language, with its definitions of terms, became the normal starting point for linguistics as well as psychology. The political role of speech was treated as secondary, as built on an already existing language. But speech originates in a group through the names with which its members are addressed! Names are not words. With words we speak of things; we speak to people by names.

The king who is crowned, the President who is inaugurated, give their name to time. Their reign covers the years with the one name in whose authority all statutes are enacted, all postal stamps and coins printed, and all school children's chronology fixed. The greatest event of any political group is the ceremony by which a "namegiver" is instituted.

Long before people had legislators like Moses or Solon, they had namegivers. *Nomos* and *onoma* (order and name), are related terms in many languages for the obvious reason that by their name leaders imparted order to time.

He who gives his name to the time of his group allows this group to cooperate in a reasoned and articulate direction. Any chieftain of a tribe is the namegiver's successor. The *Heros eponymos* of Greek tradition is called explicitly the namegiving founder after whom a city calls itself. But we are usually presented with a purely sentimental or etymological meaning of *eponymos* in our pictures of antiquity. The daily processes which emanate from a namegiver are overlooked.

Man had eras long before the Egyptians found the sky to be inscribed with an eternal calendar. These eras were inscribed in men. The head of the tribe received dress and tattoo, since his time of office served as the calendar of his people. Revolving time was measured by the chieftain's lifetime. British laws still follow this Anglo-Saxon tradition.

Researchers have erroneously looked to the traditions of primeval clans for the great astro-political calendars of the empires. Genuine clans were and are strangely uninterested in astronomy. Of course they quite often have absorbed Egyptian or Babylonian calendar-lore. This lore was superimposed on the "time-constitution" created by chieftains, but their investiture with the power to give a name to rolling time remained the true basis of tribal peace and order.

Power was given to the man who succeeded the one who had made such a name for himself that his grave held the people spellbound. A name is a result when it is self-made. A name is the freedom of office when it is bestowed. All names may be fruit and seed at the same time. We may be sure that names were enunciated and bestowed in the dirge of funerals and in the hymns of enthronment. Of course the chants were one and the same process, under the two aspects of past and of future.

The power to connect more than one generation is not given in nature. It can be lost. In 1702 Cotton Mather complained in his *Magnalia Dei* that America was in danger of becoming *res unius aetatis*, a matter of one age, and by 1922 Chesterton thought so again. The United States has always had trouble with living in many generations. The wish to continue despite death is the central problem of politics. Therefore the incision made by the death of the headman was the point of crystallization for formal speech. If this death could be overcome, the danger of becoming *res unius aetatis* was conquered. Funeral rites celebrate this conquest! In primitive society, to this day, women burst out in despair at a death, but men rise to the occasion. They build a tomb, proclaiming the dead man's name and invest the power of this man's name in a successor; graves and dresses condition each other. All dresses are the uniforms of successors to people whose names have been recognized after their death or resignation from office. They are names bestowed on successors connecting a before and a hereafter.

## 8. Ritual

Now the polarity of dress and speech is the polarity of before and after. The same life must be invested in its aspect of being in the future and remembered in its aspect of having passed away. Man cannot survive unless he constantly fits himself into new patterns. Hence investment and recording are two indispensable acts of his life on earth. Obviously there must be permanent expressions for these acts. In their unity of dress and speech, we call them ritual. In their polarity, we call them ceremonies and the events of history. What a man has done is documented by the monuments and memories, the eulogies and obituaries, he provokes. What men may do we convey by the ceremonies and formalities of their inaugurations. If man were defined at birth as a definite character, he could go naked and would not be in need of formalities. Since he is undefinable before his character as a temporal organ stands revealed at the end of his life, we need forms to protect his indefiniteness at the beginning of his career. Forms give freedom to our undefined creative powers before we have made our contribution. After we have made a name for ourselves, monuments give power to our personal contribution to the organization of life on this planet.

Human life is neither naked nor anonymous. It is ritualistic. It attains completion in its ceremonies and monuments. Our natural body does not enter the social function. We enter the social body through dress which represents a temporary body.

Analyzing these two elements as to their linguistic significance shows that they are dialectically opposed: At a funeral, upon erection of a monument, in the writing of a biography, the man who has lived makes others pronounce and remember his name. His person becomes a voice in their books, speeches or celebrations. To have made a name for yourself means literally to make other people talk and think of you! Through his recorders a person speaks to posterity, to the world.

The opposite order prevails at any ordination or inauguration. A ceremony investing a man with a function or a degree or crediting him with any power is eloquent in its attempt to make the candidate listen. Every psychological means is used to make him listen. Where the investment is placed as early as baptism, godfather and godmother are made to listen, and a lasting gift — a silver cup, a golden ring — are placed in the cradle. A cake would be a highly irrelevant gift at baptism. The great venture of baptism consists in the attempt to speak impressively to this child over his or her first twenty years. It takes quite some courage to try to make yourself heard over twenty years, but baptism attempts just this. The ceremony performed is meant to form the hearing and to draw the attention and to awaken the understanding of a child over his whole period of growth.

Funeral and baptism are ambitious. They are therefore very near the origin of speech. They deal with considerable "befores" and "afters." Baptism addresses twenty years of childhood. A whole life speaks to the world in a monument or an obituary. In these two forms, we are still able to take the "original" measure of language. Dresses are the investments of full lifetimes on credit; names are the fruits of full lifetimes lived. In these timespans, we must search for the original processes of speech. Ritual created the durability of speech. Human articulate speech bursts forth where men are initiated or buried because these lifetime ordinations are the real tasks which people face who try to end war, depression, degeneration or revolution.

A ritual cannot be taken quite seriously nor will it be formally at its best where it is applied to short-term living. It becomes humorous. The much-recommended sense of humor is unfailingly at work where long-term rites cover short-term arrangements. One cannot afford the ceremonies of an ordination for working one week in a factory. With such an attitude, the wedding ceremony becomes "for better, for divorce," or "from bed to worse." In our historical reality, rituals are everywhere cheapened by increasingly being used for brief stages of life. This process leads to vulgarization and secularization. It rendered the later Egyptian mysteries of Horus and Set farcical. It gave the Homeric gods their ironical and poetical touch. The real fullblooded ritual has often been analyzed on the basis of such late and farcical documents. They reflect the good humor of late stages when the form no longer is one of life and death. They may be compared to nursery rhymes and fairy tales which also were once fixed in truth. For this very reason these late documents often hamper our understanding of speech. Words are like axes and swords before humor takes the edge off them. For the verbal ritual sweeps clean long alleys of time into the future and into the past, lest a man's life remain subhuman. It is a law that man is not human unless determined physical organization and undetermined social organ — or man's body and his temporal character — are integrated into unity. Ritual, which consists of ceremonial and named memory, is the process for this integration. For this reason, ritual is measured in generations; the yard-stick of a ritual's perfection is its power to tie together whole generations of men. A ritual that does less is second rate and cannot help us interpret the rituals of primary importance.

To interpret this primary ritual we may do well to concentrate on the question of power. Cutting out alleys of thirty or forty years into the future and into the past takes power. It takes much more power than we attribute to speech. The vulgar philosophy of language tells us that speech communicates one man's thought to another. But our opinions are ephemeral. If speech were intended to convey ideas, it would need as little power as possible. And it is true, our modern speakers lisp nearly tonelessly; they prefer to write form letters on a typewriter or send out mimeographed charts and statistics. They try to make as little noise as possible. They are right. Who am I that my opinions, thoughts or ideas should inconvenience anybody else? They live their faith in their philosophy of language. But their philosophy of language interprets secondary types of speech. It does not even try to interpret the monumental character of names. It believes with Kant that "time" is a form of thought.

History and our own experience in great calamity prove that time is created by speech. We may all be in time before we speak. But we have time solely because we can distinguish a present between the past and the future. Now this present exists nowhere in nature, but we can create it by uniting in a name and by pooling our diverse lifetimes into one great reservoir of supertime. Man has as much time as he has names under which generations of men are willing to cooperate through the ages. We enjoy a present when we have joined hands with others of other times, past and future, in one spirit.

The first present, then, is the extant moment between a name which illuminates past years of performance and a title destined to illuminate future years of succession to this performance. There is a distinct relation between this past and this future. The more we honor the names of the past, the more claim do we lay to a long future. It is a frequent misunderstanding to treat these two aspects of time as of different length or as mutual impediments. Past and future are corollaries to such an extent that human speech always embraces them in one name which unfolds backward and forward at the same time. The ceremonies of a state funeral and a state inauguration proclaim the great truth that we produce our future by constant renaissances of the past. The entire history of the race forever tries to recover all lived life. He who does not honor his past has no future. This is the essence of conscious living. It articulates times and places as between past and future so convincingly that we receive a clear direction and orientation as to our place in time.

The chieftain who is hoisted on his predecessor's shield thereafter speaks in the authority of his name. When I speak in somebody's name, I speak his tongue. The new head of a group speaks a tongue. This tongue is his followers'. These terms would tell the truth about formal speech loudly if only we would stop and listen to them. The tongue which is the "mother tongue" through the millennia and the "head," as the chieftain is called from generation to generation, are symbolical expressions. Here is not a physical head but a leader, and the tongue is a group idiom; it is a speech which centers around a perpetual namegiving office.

The last century has separated the treatment of "heads" and "tongues." The mother tongue was a nationalistic, sentimental topic of "English." "Heads" were left to anthropology. But both condition one another. The mother tongue is nothing but the experience of a group which receives and accepts names above itself through a creative and present-day process vested in a head. The mother tongue and the paternal head, when torn apart, become scourges of superstition.[14] Our nationalism has introduced a form of mother worship without fatherhood, a kind of virgin birth for our respective languages!

Nationalism expanded on the spirit of national literature and lore as though these had come about without political decisions, loyalties or commotions. Nationalism interpreted language as a nation's natural endowment.

Today we see whole languages explode. After 1933 Hitler's Germany exhaled sounds which betrayed a demonic spirit to anybody whose mother tongue was German. Later times will describe the decomposition of German under Hitler as the first great observable case of the death of a language in a short period of time. On the other hand, artificial languages are invented, like basic English, Esperanto, etc. The Nazis passed laws on language in their hubris of establishing themselves. In our own times, death and artifact turn language into an arena of political and economic interests.

Therefore we should try to recognize the origins of speech. Our diagnosis of present-day disorder would be insufficient without such an analysis.

The first result of our analysis is that heads and tongues were made to speak in the name of buried heroes. Heads ceremoniously bestowed the namegivers' authority on those who wore them as their social body. Dress gave title and rank in the community for a lifetime or for a limited length of time. In this way periods were hewn out in the thicket of time, during which the invested person was free to wield the power bestowed upon him. All freedom is power for the future. The necessity to create successors to leaders created title to freedom.

When we moderns say "every man a king" or "every man a priest," we do not say that there are no kings or no priests, although the vulgar acceptance of these phrases might suggest this meaning. We say that at long last everybody has attained the freedom of priests and kings. The universal priesthood of all believers and the general royalty of all citizens confirms our discovery that freedom and power come through office or function. It is a gift of the social body to its members. Democracy, it is true, tries to extend the freedom of the highest offices, of priests or kings, of speakers and of scribes, to all. However, without the degrees of priest and king, nothing would be extended to all.

In the economy of the future our slogan may well become: "every man a chief," that is: every man a foreman who can give orders in the factory and not only receive them. How far are we, however, from the slogan: "every man a chief"? We had 10 million people who were without a boss before Pearl Harbor. Will not for a long period the cry for a job come first, which is in truth the cry for somebody to tell me what to do for wages? But this means that we all cluster desperately around the totem pole of some product which may be sold at a profit. We who have achieved the recognition that all men may act as priests and kings will have a long road to travel before the economy of the future will have room for the imperative: "everybody a chief!" We should cherish this as the ultimate goal. In the meantime, we will need the captains of industry, we will need lieutenant-commanders and more and more ships, lest one half of us fall prey to the jungle of unemployment, of no commands for us whatsoever. We are in search of chiefs.

In church I may well be captain of my soul; but captain of my daily bread? The wizards of Social Justice, Social Credit, Social Millennium, National

Socialism, the Corporate State and Social Insurance climb the hustings of our days because we look to them in our fear of unemployment. At a meeting of 70 educators in May 1940, a speaker defined a citizen of the U.S. as "a man who is profitably employed." I was the only one present who protested; the other men did not understand my protest. So much has this mighty republic changed since the Civil War. Then a citizen was a man who could become President or Governor or Judge. In other words citizens governed. When 70 educators can call a citizen a man who is profitably employed, we must have lost interest or faith or hope in government and must be concentrating on orders for work. This is the change from kings to chiefs, from citizens to job hunters, from empires to clans, from constitutional conventions about lawgiving to cooperative fellowships about giving orders. Power over the future is in the hands of those fellows who can provide jobs, and that means order.

This is of course one of the reasons for learning to think more correctly about speech and dress at this juncture. For it is power over the future which is entrusted by dress and speech, always. Those who were inaugurated as heirs of a noble and renowned past were created (in Latin, *creare heredem!*) through ceremonies. Not birth but formal acceptance of his heir by the father created the heir.

In any ceremony, dress is used as the creator of a new "spiritual," social body for the man who wears that dress. Through names conjured up in speaking at the graves the mantle of the past falls upon the shoulders of successors.

Speech surges in the seam between death and birth. Somebody must have lived "successfully" before he can be succeeded explicitly. Caesar had to be murdered before people recognized the immortality of the office of a Caesar. The realism of speech is that it comes after the darknesses of common living and personal suffering. Caesar murdered, Christ crucified, Egypt abandoned, Cain outcast, the Persians expelled — these processes beget new speech.

The history of all law makes it appear more probable that our interpretation of this seam between death and birth is correct. The first and originally the only law is the law of succession. The two codes, the penal and the civil, depend on the difference between a violent death or a natural death. In nearly all languages complaint in court for a violent death and *planctus*, formal mourning for natural death are called by the same or related names.

Nearly all non-Christian civilizations preserve the bursting forth of legal and formal complaint out of natural and animal wails. Women are expected to contribute the wild, passionate, inarticulate shouts of blind feeling. Men are expected to build on this natural stratum the structure of high and articulate speech. The Dionysian rites as well as the professional mourners among the Jews of the Polish ghettos divide these functions. Women and children yell, weep, shake; men act and speak.

This division of labor seems to prove that we are here faced with an important law of history: a new ritual, created as the victory over a negative aspect of life, consists of the acts and gestures, the sounds and words by which the appearance of order out of chaos, of shape out of confusion, can be re-lived each time the ritual is enacted. The negative situation which precedes is made part of the ritual lest the positive solution which follows remain incomprehensible. Rituals whose pre-history, whose "irritation" is no longer understandable, fail to move us. Reverence for man's power to speak depends on our fear of being plunged into the animal state. Women may manipulate speech like men among us. But at the beginning of our era, and as I said, outside the vital Christian development, this was and is not the case. In these strata the human race is still busy representing the process from yell to speech by enacting the proceedings through which this emergence is achieved.

The spirit proceeds in the interaction between the women and children, on the one hand and the men on the other. This is the meaning of the term "process of the spirit." The modern mind has not much use for this creative term — it might speak of "emergence from chaos." However, the word emergence misses the central point of ritual. We emerge from the water, from a shock, from a dizzy spell, but the elements out of which we emerge are left behind. Emergence is a natural process, and in nature the individual and its environment are looked at as separate entities. The opposite attitude prevails in ritual: wails are transsubstantiated and speech proceeds out of the very origins, the sounds which made up the wails. For thousands of years when a murder was committed, the relatives of the slain man were required to carry the corpse before the judges. In open court, the complaint was made by the womens' lamentation as well as by accusation from the mouth of the next of kin.

This dualism made the *concentus* of our animal nature and our formal history transparent. Man cried first and spoke afterwards, because to speak was the first step away from the cry. Cries and shouts were inserted in the ceremony as the yardstick of articulate speech. This interaction of shout and name, of woman and man in religion, was the great reconciliation between our animal and our intellectual nature. When Paul asked that women be silent in church he said it at a time and within a world in which the women — Jewish and Gentiles alike — were expected to utter terrible wails and yells, to be Sibyls and Bacchants, to utter passionate cries at any funeral. The modern detractors of Paul usually have not the faintest idea what they attack. Paul made formal speech accessible to women by freeing them from the burden of pre-Christian ritual in which they strewed ashes on their heads, punctured their breasts and uttered long-drawn cries for days. Paul was faced with passionate people who stammered and had fits under the new dispensation of freedom, who had been obsessed by spirits and by demons of their clan or family.

Paul's *taceat mulier* laid the foundations of a new truth that women may from now on participate in the word as well as men. And his command has been successful. We no longer fear that we shall hear hysterical cries in church. Women behave as respectably in religious gatherings as though they were men. And now, women scold Paul's backwardness. Let them ask themselves if, after Hitler, they can deny the existence of man's animal nature. Is relapse into hysterics impossible? Is a ritual in which the spirit proceeds and in which we ourselves mourn that we have killed the son of God, incomprehensible? If "hysteria" and if animal nature have disappeared for good, we no longer need ritual. When no children are born and the last generation lives immortally forever, we could drop ritual. Ritual insists that all our attainments in history are established on the elementary foundations of our animal beginnings. Therefore nothing lasts in history which is not incessantly reestablished. Languages are not "born." Man must learn to speak as he must learn to write. The child's speech and the student's writing are but small fragments of the powers bestowed on man by the tribal ritual.

The tribal ritual communicated religion, law, writing and speech. Ritual created time — as past and future, power — as freedom and succession, order — as title and name, expectation — as ceremony and dress, tradition

— as dirge and the myth of the hero. It bound man into time. This is expressed by the term "religion." We will devote a special section to the tragedy of such "bounds." Indeed, the binding powers of tribal religion became cruel fetters. I am certainly not blind to this cruelty. The best is always the seat of the most terrible corruption. But first the tribe must be evaluated positively, in its greatness, namely such greatness that we learned to speak at all.

Evolutionists cannot do justice to this greatness since they take speech for granted. He who sees whole strata of life become speechless and relapse into dumbness or civil war admires the attainment by which we can speak. Of course the perpetual pro-cessus by which animal sounds can be trans-substantiated into speech was and is only possible when the whole soul of men, male and female, enters the pro-cessus. Only that is important to which both men and women contribute.

But ritual is of exactly this character. It is based on the clash of two natures, feminine and masculine. And on this basis, it establishes an order which tries to last forever. Ritual forever enacts the first victory over speechlessness. Ritual created a lasting order far beyond the moment.

As we perceive the relation between the holy hours of ritual and the long-range future, another hitherto incomprehensible aspect of language may be grasped. Invariably, people think that some man one day began to call the head "head," the hand "hand," then afterwards, the word got into the dictionary and was used happily ever after. The opposite is true. Before our era no word ever got into the dictionary unless it was used in ritual. In those days, no word was a word unless it had first been inaugurated as a holy name. Forget-me-nots were not "forget-me-nots," reeds not "reeds," oaks not "oaks," before the chieftain or medicine man had addressed them in public ritual and asked them to participate. Flowers and animals, fire and water, trees and stones, were spoken to in ritual before anybody ever spoke of them. Hence, when they were addressed in any human tongue for the first time, they received full names and not empty words.

Cubs and their mother may point to a nut or a stick, they may shout with joy in their play over this and that, there and here. Hither and thither they turn for food, toys and weapons. But no name is the result of all this life of the moment.

Ritual is needed to create a language which will go down through fifty or a hundred and fifty generations. Such language is essential for a ritual. The relation of any ritual to time is that of one hour or day to the whole past which it reveals in its names and to the whole future which it veils by its ceremonious dress. Ritual was made as long as possible because it enacts the forever and forever. Ritual supposedly creates a lasting order, far beyond the moment. The task of forming a time cup of promise and fulfillment seemed stupendous. The tribe might celebrate three days or a week. But the fact remained that the meetings ultimately had to disband; people had to go home. The ritual's problem was to compensate for this loss of continuity and physical presence. Speech and dress became the representatives of the ritual for the rest of the time when the tribe was not assembled. The deficiency of ritual is that, compared to the timespans which it tries to embrace, its own proceedings never are long enough. Hence it created lasting representations. It was so successful that we still speak the languages of six thousand years ago. Languages are immortal because they aimed at immortality!

But would we say "chief," "tongue," "hand," "crown," "pole," and "fire" if some child had said so to its mother? Certainly not. The words which we speak today were not at first technical tools of communication. They were sacred names and powers, rights and laws, curses and blessings, friends and foes. The modern words "chief," "crown," "hand," "tongue," etc. were originally called upon as names of a short ceremony which organized long times. In order to impress the right of a hero's successor upon his people, he was crowned, was made a head, and was ascribed the hero's tongue. A mask was set upon him. Every Roman triumphant general wore the red mask of Romulus. He spoke another man's "tongue" and wore another man's "head."

From the very beginning both these terms were used symbolically. Nobody would need a definite name for head or tongue as long as he can point to one with his finger or stick the other out. But ceremonies need names because a physical thing is used to point out a political order. Formal language came into being as sacred ritual. Every word spoken pointed beyond the physical or "objective" to the political and religious meaning. Speech did not name the materials of nature; it did name the historical roles of men and things as they appeared to the "thing" or *thingus* of the tribe. A kidney was called a "kidney," a liver was called a "liver," and a tongue a "tongue" because all these terms were sacred names at their origin. The origin of speech is sacramental. "Things," physical things, were used to express a new order introduced by the power of dead leadership. The "tongue" was a sacrament by which the new leader stood in authority when he raised his voice. The "liver" was the seat of genius and of suffering. The "head" was the tribe's head when the great mask was placed upon the head of the new chief. The "testicles" testified to the regeneration of life. Every name served as a sacrament by which the momentary physical act established lasting political actuality.

We usually say that seven or nine were used as sacred numbers. They probably were not used in a sacred manner but rather like all other names — they were sacred at the very first because the ritual repeated certain acts three or nine or seven times. The oldest parts of the *zendavesta* of the Persians gives wonderful examples of a language in which words did not exist but which was composed of names. Butter and water, milk and fire, air and wind, all are persons to whom the praying leader speaks. He can never really speak of them as objects in words. They are more real to him than he himself. He realizes himself solely by giving all of them the right names and by simultaneously moving through them in the right order. In this ritual of names, new names spring up for new acts, incessantly.

No act is admitted into civilization unless a ritual declares it to have been scrutinized and found acceptable. The terms for our processes of cooking (frying, stewing, braising, etc.) mentioned earlier were admitted as specific forms of sacrificial burnt offerings in the ritual. In Arabia, to this day, certain meats may only be cooked at gatherings of the whole tribe, while others are allowed to the single family. Even the foodstuffs were so much part of the political ritual. Animals had always been included, and man was close to them.

When man's families became secure, he learned to domesticate bulls, and used the same term for the act of castration as for chastity. For castration was as much a religious ceremony as marriage. I knew an old Catholic cook who never slaughtered a chicken without first saying: "God bless the chicken." This Christian form has superseded the priestly ritual for the butchering of geese and ducks which we still can read on the temple walls of Egypt. Our forms of grammar are residues of ritual. Even the minor professions of baker, miller and smith needed ritual. The technical processes of lighting fire, churning butter, ploughing and hunting needed recognition of their names before they were admitted as legal into the tribe's peace.

Ritual was repetitive; it may be called the permanent calisthenics of a social body in formation. The members inhaled the order of the tribe's organization through speech and dress in ceremonies.

## 9. Grammar and Ritual

If the above outline is true, the logic of sentences must correspond to the structure of ritual. In a previous section, this logic unfolded as second person, first person, third person, verbal noun through imperatives, lyrical mood, narratives and judgments. Is the scheme – *i, eamus, ierunt, ire* – a process which is recognizable in ritual? It becomes recognizable as soon as we face the whole group, the dead, the listeners as well as the speakers. Indeed, the inhalation of order by the listeners through the speakers from the dead produces the grammatical situations which are basic to formal speech. When the ritual begins, listeners are made as important as speakers: they march in and bow deep; they lie prostrate, or they kneel. They are asked to harken and to obey. This process is so preponderant that the mood of the gathering is determined more by the attitude of an excited audience ready to hear than by the speaker himself. The greatest impression of act one of a ritual is usually that a voice is going to speak to us. In any poignant ritual, the gathering must be conceived as the second person of grammar, the person being spoken to.

Grammatically speaking, there is no "I" in the imperative; there is a "thou" in every listener's heart. Scientific psychology begins with an ego and then adds "he's" and an "it" to its inventory. But the real story of the human spirit always begins by our assimilating an imperative. We understand that we are meant, and in doing what our mother asks us to do we realize ourselves for the first time as our mother's – or our father's or our teacher's – "thou" and "you." I am a thou for society long before I am an I to myself. This proper order of the soul's grammatical persons is found in all ritual. "We" as humans are not the speakers but "you" are made to listen. Ritual emphasizes that the power which makes anybody in the assembly speak is superhuman. The only ego is God. And since the tribesmen experience God in moments of agony, death and bereavement, the spirit of the dead man speaketh, the living listen. We are vocatives, not nominatives, in our own experience of ourselves. To this day health of mind depends on this relation between listening first and becoming a speaker later. As we have found before, man's grammar is "thou" first and "I" second. Everybody, in listening, can be spoken to by the spirit. The spirit pervades us in the process of our being formed; and inspired we begin to sing and to dance. This is act two of ritual. Since no scientific dogma here blocks the road, every reader will know dozens of examples of lyrics, ballet and chorus.

Thereupon the story is told, the myth of the hero. He is represented: his mask, his power, his deeds. He is buried, he is mourned. Act three.

The forms are then repeated − three times, four times and more. And either a solemn prologue, a herald or an announcer may say this formally. The end is also stated with great care. *Ite, missa est.* This cryptic formula of dismissal at Mass connects us with primeval ritual in its fourth phase of objectivation.

Whole lifetimes were enacted on such occasions and therefore all creatures had an opportunity to be called up. A variety of holidays was introduced. Whenever a new holiday was needed, new and sometimes contradictory processes had to be sanctioned for use in the community. Today we dig out the potsherds of primitives, the fragments of tombs thousands of years old. We are unearthing the cemeteries of the past. But it is the heavenly order of ritual which lies buried there. The bones which we unearth, the flintstones, are not simply part of corpses or of quarries; they are the fossils of speech and ritual. These are not chemical or biological facts but "the life of life," the order which results when death precedes birth and the end gives origin to the beginning.

We still live today by these same stages of ritual. They still keep us organized. Art, science, law, religion, sports and education now form the great rituals and grammar of society. And they should move us, as all men have been moved through all times, through the same phases of "harken" of "thou-ness," to the lyrics of subjects, the epics of biographical history, and finally to the arithmetic of numerical objectivity.

But, as in all times, many men in our days do not fully participate in this ritual. Let nobody think that our languages are anything but potsherds to most men. Webster's dictionary lists so many words. It is a cemetery of potsherds. All these words by which we may talk of anything under the sun were once glorious names sung in prayer, pronounced in ritual, and inspiring man to action. At some time, none of these words could be uttered without making a whole society move, kneel, cook, march, shout, kill, dance, embrace or obey.

The potsherds of ancient speech which are now left are the words we are free to use without taking action. Law, poetry, religion and history are expected to take care of the life of great names. We ourselves try to live in shirt sleeves as the low brow and cultivate slang. Who can be serious day and night? Indeed we can't. Let us not be sentimental. Informal, pronominal speech, through nose and throat, has replaced the full tones of plain chant, from chest and rump, in which man first spoke. We use "this" and "that," "anyhow" and "so what?" for right and wrong, God and inspiration. But a little story from the Bell Company may serve to remind us of the actual existence of formal speech even among us and of its vicissitudes, in the East and in the West.

An experiment made by the Bell Telephone Company sheds light on "formal" and "informal" speech. When they taught their operators to speak slowly "thththrrreee," instead of three, they unknowingly went back to plainsong, the formal speech of old. To offset the austerity of such formal sounds, the company hit on the way in which one of the Eastern nations, the Chinese, have withdrawn their daily life from the severity of formal speech. The Chinese still use the modulations of plainsong in their light tones. They have no pronouns and yet they are not formal for they smile; by smiling, we make sounds soft and he who smiles is in phonetic slippers, so to speak. A Chinese is informal by smiling as we are by using pronouns! The American Bell Company actually requires its employees to smile while they speak with increased precision. In this manner, the East's informal speech without pronouns was rediscovered here in America.

## 10. Question and Answer

We have not spoken of one form of speech which prevails in many grammars for people who wish to learn a foreign language: "What is this thing? – This thing is a nail." "Who is this man? – This man is my father." The game of question and answer is so predominant in modern language teaching that we had better analyze the responsory which it represents. Does it refute our theses about the ritual of speech? Not all questions are alike. Question and answer in the above examples, as we shall see, are of a secondary nature in the ritual. On the other hand, there are dramatic questions which may belong to an oath, a vow, an ordeal, and seem to have a ritualistic character.

Let us first look at the kind of question which is common among us, that which simply asks for information. This will clarify the action character of speech by underlining the contrast. The analysis will show that questions and answers prepare us for participation in the movements of society. "Thou shalt honor thy father and mother," "This road is the highway to Paris," may be transformed into questions as follows:

```
      (who)
        ?         shalt honor father and mother.
a.
      (which)
        ?         road is the highway to Paris.


              will
      Thou  ? can    honor father and mother.
              must
b.
              path
      This  ? river  is the highway to Paris.
              trail


                  honor
      Thou shalt  ? obey       father and mother.
                  love
c.
      This road    ? was        the highway to Paris.
                   will become


                        grandmother
      Thou shalt honor  ? sister      and mother.
                        daughter
                        uncle
d.
                        one
      This road is      ? no         highway to Paris.
                        the nearest
```

|  | or |  |  |
|---|---|---|---|
| Thou shalt honor father ? | more than | mother. |  |
|  | no more than |  |  |

e.

|  | detour |  |  |
|---|---|---|---|
| This road is the ? | gateway to | Paris |  |
|  | railroad |  |  |

|  | brothers |
|---|---|
|  | ancestors |
| Thou shalt honor father and ? | family |
|  | sons |

f.

|  | London |
|---|---|
| This road is the highway to ? | New York |
|  | Versailles |

These questions point to an uncertainty of the speaker about one link in the sentence. He himself cannot say the whole sentence before he has found the missing part of the cadence. The whole sentence stands in his mind all ready to be said; he is blocked by the gap of one word in it. The answer fills this gap. Once the answer is given, the speaker is able to say with assurance: "The fourth commandment says: Thou shalt honor father and mother. This is the highway to Paris."

The question is preliminary. It prepares a man to speak or to think and thereby to know a sentence of which he stands in need either for recitation or for meditation. Once these questions are answered, a person is able to participate in the intellectual process of society. He is, as the French beautifully say, *mis au courant*. He now can share in the "current" of events.

The child who learns the ten commandments or the stranger who wishes to behave like a native find their way into communal life through these questions. These questions rest on existing patterns of a community's language and introduce to it new members who learn the precise elements of the established speech. The questions prepare participation. This stands

revealed when we look at this form. We may write out the questions
formally as:

———— ? ———— ———— ? ———— ? ———— ————

———— ———— ———— ? ———— ————

———— ———— ———— ———— ? ————

The word in question is not pronounced but instead a "what," or a "who," a
*quis, quo, quantum* is inserted, some empty form, a mere shell. Perhaps it is
better to say that the speaker gives us to understand that he is, for this one
part of the sentence, completely openminded. He is in a plastic mood and
throws his tongue, for this part at least, into the plastic mold of the answer.

A question entrusts the restoration of the whole sentence to somebody
else, and for this reason the part in question is spoken *sotto voce*, in a subdued
and half articulated manner. The question is like the "la la la" in a song of
which we do not know the text. But we could not ask the question if there
were no song or sentence to be restored. For this simple reason, certain
questions make no sense. One cannot say "why do the masses howl?"
because the only thing men who are condemned to form a mob might ask is
that they be allowed to cease being a mob. There is no why in a mob's
behavior. "What does the world plan?" is an idiot's question. The world may
perhaps be planned, but we call "the world" that aspect of the universe in
which it appears as an object of our mind and therefore the world itself cannot plan.

"Is there a God?" is a similarly stupid question. God is the speaking voice,
the power to speak. Since I ask a question, I already am dominated by this
power. The questions "what do the masses want?," "what does the world
plan?," "is there a God?" have no cadence for which they search. For the
masses, insofar as they are a mob, know of no cause. The world insofar as it
is the world, has no purpose. God insofar as he is the pure act of speech has
no visible existence.

Previous to the questions – Why do these masses howl?, What does the
world plan?, Is there a God? – we have already heard it said: "this is a mob,
which is negative (mobs act without reason); "this is the world," which is objective (the world moves by law, without purpose); "this is true," which is an
act of faith (I trust myself). These questions therefore stand condemned as
pseudo-questions because they do not prepare us for participation in the

restored mental life of the community. They do not restore a preestablished sentence!

But in ritual there is a question of a somewhat different character. A novice might thrice be asked to answer a certain solemn question, and thrice he may have to answer it ceremoniously. The answer is examined and tried by these questions. The context of the sentence is not diffuse like "la, la, la," but the answer seems to require encouragement; he needs to be brought to his full presence of mind. These questions try to compel a speaker to become fully conscious of the sentence which is laid before him; these questions fight against lipservice. The oath, the ordeal, the vow have this character of digging out a man's innermost conviction, his lasting relation to this statement. And so we find the great answers of "yea," of "no," of "amen." We find pledges, collaterals, mortgages, hostages. They all try to reply to the question: "Do you mean it?"

As has rightly been said: "Human life must be a living affirmation of the truth." From the beginning of time speech has looked for forms to clothe a person's entire life in the truth. The ending of the first person singular in Latin and Greek – *amo, dico, lego,* and in Germanic – *sago, gebo* – is composed with an affirmative exclamation such as we have in oh yes and oh no. The "first person" in a man's attitude appeared in grammar under the pressure of an oath, an ordeal, a wedding promise – it was not a proposition of abstract truth, but the explicit voluntary decision to warrant a truth with one's personal life-time. "These are ten thousand sheep," may be true or not. Who knows? But if you ask me for statements as weighty as: "I say," "I swear," "I promise," "I do," they are promises backed by a man's lifetime of responsibility. For this reason their grammatical form differs so widely from the third person's indicative. "I am" and "he is" are completely different.

In modern English, the inflections of the verb having nearly disappeared, all the charm of grammar has retired into the spelling. Hence, if we wish to understand the treatment of the first person, we will have to find our significance in its spelling. Just as "borrow" and "borough," "waive" and "wave," "root" and "route," live on as separate forms on account of the secrets of spelling, so the first person singular of the verb continues to lead a moral existence of its own with the help of the capital letter used for i. It is indeed important that a man should pledge his word for a truth. He is a God who vouchsafes the truth with his whole life, or who backs his promise with all he has. The "I" of God is imparted to a man who takes an oath. He associates with the gods when he opens his lips to say: "But I tell you."

Any scientist who announces a discovery is expected to stake his whole reputation on his description of it. And what is the result? They produce electric dynamos in a town in New Jersey called "Ampere," and we measure by "Volts" and "Watts." Science has given those "I"s who have staked their whole reputation on a truth the power to become lasting names for their truth. Let nobody imagine that this usage of science is its own invention. The solemnities of science continue usages of former times. People always felt in contact with the divine when they dared to say: "I." When they feel like mortals, they say meekly: "me" or "myself," not "I." A famous autobiography has the title: "Me." Could it be "I"? To recapitulate: questions which ask for my degree of seriousness do not revive an established sentence; they demand a new witness to truth from the person who is required to answer. The witness is cast into the statement as metal is poured into a mold. His deposition commits his future behavior because he must stand behind his words.

Is there a third set of questions and answers? Don't we doubt the truth? Don't we doubt the Gods? It is all very well to say that the question, "Is there a God?," is nonsense. But are we not provoked to say terrible and nonsensical things?

It may sound strange, but the authentic place for the most tantalizing questions is in prayer. If it is sincere, all prayer is doubtful, agitated, despairing, searching. The cold residue of prayer is nowadays called "research." If research is real, it still has the dignity of prayer, although it is the last and most cooled-off phase of genuine prayer. Prayer does not question the parts of a sentence of the first type, nor does it question the partnership of an answer of the second type. It questions the authenticity of the questioner himself! Prayer asks: "What is man that thou should be mindful of him?" or "Who am I, the questioner?" "Am I, am I not ephemeral, shadow of shadows swayed by the day," Pindar said. "But when one ray of light comes down out of the sky-god's quiver, everything is easy, and blissful is man's era."

An invocation is meant to restore the questioner, to give him full stature, direction and orientation in his ritual. Prayer directs, illuminates, establishes him who has to speak with authority. We all are priests under the condition that we all intend to say something. Priesthood is the right obtained by prayer to speak with a claim to being followed and obeyed. The invocation of that spirit by which I have the unquestionable or – after doubt – the re-established right to speak, has been replaced in modern society by the "introduction" of a speaker. This ceremony – one of the most interesting among the ceremonies of our unceremonious society – reflects all the original features of an invocation: "Who is the speaker?" is the question asked by the chairman or master of ceremonies. And he puts the speaker in the rightful place of authority where he belongs before he can expect to be listened to.

In churches a responsory between the minister and the congregation puts him in the right spirit. The minister says: "The Lord be with you." The congregation responds: "And with thy spirit."

This is a purification of the ancient invocation by the priest. In the church, through his prayer for the community, he forgets himself in his concern for his neighbors; then, by the gracious and free gift of these neighbors, the spirit is invoked over him. Fittingly, this respondence takes place before he opens his mouth for the sermon. When a college teacher gets up before a class, there is nowadays no special invocation. But he is in the chair under the school's auspices. This means that the institution represents the invocation permanently. Emphasis on the community's assistance and contribution for a man's authority to speak is universal; an unexpected example may be quoted from the Osage Indians. The tribe's riders sing: "Our brave young men have found in me their leader; I go forth in obedience to their call." Or they sing: "Many are the valiant men abler than I to command, yet it is I you have called. Courageous, dauntless are our foes, you say, yet it is I upon whom you call."[15]

The call for the leader, the calling of the priest, whether it surges from the visible congregation or from the invisible, establishes the speaker as a real speaker. The oath of allegiance converts acting people into true listeners. The search for correct expression in the rite gives the final statement its dignity. Three truths may be doubted every time we speak. And all three doubts have their ritual. We behave strangely in that we relegate the ritual acts for the three truths and their three doubts to separate watertight compartments. Self-doubt of speakers we deal with in religion or ceremony. Self-doubt of listeners is dealt with in the laws about oaths, mortgages, hostages in war time, etc.; the content of the spoken sentence we analyze in logic.

I cannot admit that this is appropriate. All three aspects of truth explain each other. It may be less subtle and less refined to deal with them in their unity as I have done here. I admit my shortcomings. But all the subtleties of logic, law or religion will not help us until we reunite the three aspects or the three doubts and see them as one. Any ritual, and therefore all formal speech, tries to insure the authority of the commander or speaker, the truthfulness of his people or listeners, and the truth of the statements to which both, commander and people, respond. Ritual and formal speech must achieve these three things.

Prayer may be too narrow or too wide a term for the invocation of the spirit by every speaker before he speaks and after he has spoken. But there is nothing mysterious, mystical or unreasonable in an invocation. It is one necessary third of the whole mental process which we call speech and which we all use. Prayer is the egress from speechless slumber and the "transgress" of a future speaker into the field of force in which "I" require to be listened to. For this reason every speaker must deal with the question: "By what right do I claim to speak at all?", "In whose name do I require your attention?" Is curiosity, vanity, justice, liberty, fair play or self interest my reason for speaking? Or is it a calling, a duty, a vision, a light, a command, which compel me to speak?

The invocations of prayer offer the third set of questions, the questions which a man asks about himself lest he forfeit his power to speak at all.

| I. *Quis* and *quid*, who and what questions | fill a gap in an established sentence |
| II. Promise, oath, pledge questions | place a witness behind his deposition |
| III. Invocations and prayer | authorize the questioner to speak "in the name of" (freedom, decency, science, poetry, truth, etc.) |

All three sets of questions illuminate once more the fact already known to us, that any sentence spoken throws light on speaker, listener, and the world outside. Therefore when this light is dimmed in any one of the three directions, it can be restored by one special set of questions.

In the ritual of speech, questions and answers have the function of restoring the flow of the drama of speech. They help strangers, novices, the illiterate, the ignorant and the forgetful to know what everybody must know if he is to participate in the movements of society.

The wonderful gain of our analysis is a better insight into the drama of speech. The three forms of questions re-establish for us the whole setting in which a human being is able to speak.

The first set of questions depends on established truth. They connect a newcomer with the accepted formulations of society. No such questions make sense except in relation to some previously enacted drama, some historical order, some past imperatives, some older feelings, former tales, told before the question is formulated. Form I is trying to enter not into a natural reality but into existing social formulations and traditions. If we ignore this, we make fools of ourselves. Most of our scientists are cut off from their logical foundations so completely that they do not know when they can ask "why?" or "what?" Such questions are nonsensical when nobody has spoken before. Unknowingly, they appeal to an authoritative statement.

If I ask: "Why do individuals form a society?," I will never get an answer. For nowhere has any community ever believed the truth that individuals form a society. It is true that some individuals who were formed by society to a high degree of liberty, who were informed into the mores of such a free society, have asked this question. It is an insipid question just the same. The very language in which it was asked exists only because these individuals sacrificed their separatedness in the ritual of speech; in the surrender of their individual nature, these individuals create a second nature common to all. Individuals cease to be individuals when they speak. The smart analyst who asks "why did they do it?" is begging the question.

The first set of questions reaffirms the time axis into an acknowledged tradition of formulated truth. Such questions presuppose the whole history of spoken life and wish to make it flow unobstructedly.

In the second set of questions the witness affirms the consequences of speech in the future. He creates a future backing today's statement. Speaking man created future, science cannot. For the future we need people who will back up our laws, our hopes, our promises. The set of questions asked at confirmation, wedding, in court, by the notary, in the army, conjure up the future of time. The answerer accepts a future life enlightened by the inspired sentence.

The third set of questions is perhaps of the greatest significance. It creates authority. But this amounts to the creation of a new dimension. What is this dimension? It is a dimension which is usually denied. But it is a dimension without which I could not write these lines nor could you, reader, read them. It is the dimension of the high and the low which does not exist before we have spoken.

We can't see this dimension today, because we can't see the forest for the trees. Everybody, we say, can speak. Oh, and everybody can write and even writes books. "Each one teach one," said the Filipino chieftain when the organized mission broke down. Since everybody speaks, we overlook the boundary line between the forest of speakers and the swamps, the deserts, the wasteland where no speech proceeds. Granted that out of 140,000,000 Americans, 50 million do vote; the other 90 million who do not vote still accept the word of those 50: they listen. And when each one teaches one, the relation is still 50:50. Every speaker needs a listener who believes that it is worthwhile to listen!

When Nietzsche composed his famous nightsong, he said: "my soul's violin sang to herself this song. Did anybody listen?" And when nobody listened, he went mad. Of course he went mad, for our speech vanishes from us unless somebody listens. And to him who listens, who obeys, who does what he is told, the speaker, the commander, the boss, must be the boss. And this hated superiority is the condition for the existence of any magazine, lecture, court, army, government, literature or theater.

The division into high and low is a condition of human speech. All the masks of democracy cannot conceal the divine character of all speech. You listen to me not because I am better or superior, but because the superior, higher, sublime, may perhaps reach you through me. The man who speaks "is" not higher, but he stands higher. A society in which nobody stands higher than anybody else is a mob. 10,000 people in one place without a platform from which a speaker can make himself heard or a principle can be established is a pitiful collection of earthly dirt.

In 1944 a modern intellectual in *The Nation* excoriated a poet who said that high and low was a more fundamental difference than left and right. This same intellectual reviewed a book by the same poet; he sat in the reviewer's chair; he wielded authority. He was placed above the crowd when he condemned the man who pointed to this very fact. And the reviewer thought nothing of hoping that General Eisenhower's authority should be obeyed by all his — terrible word — *sub*ordinates.

Turn which way you like, dear worm of man. You must get on a platform before you can become a man. High and low are products of man's faith in speech. The third set of questions examines the foundations of the platform on which any speaker must stand before the polarity "one speaks, the other listens" can be established. When the speaker asks the gods "Who am I?" and when the chairman soothes the assembly "Listen to the speaker," both times the distinction of high and low is established.

All speech creates history and future. High and low are established. In the three sets of questions they may be recreated and imparted to newcomers.

## 11. The Trivium and Symbols

The insights we have thus far gained open up three new practical roads for dealing with the "trivia" of languages, literature and logic. One road leads to a different method of teaching languages — the mother tongue as well as foreign languages. Foreign languages should first be learned as high languages before the colloquial is stressed. Songs and laws and psalms form a better starting point. The game of questions and answers might advantageously be replaced by imperatives and reports. I have composed one example, a Latin grammar, which has been used in a seminary.[16]

The second road opens into history. The various layers of speech signify great epochs in history. Just as we speak of diluvium and trias in geology, we may well come to speak of the eras of plainchant, of the separation of speech and script, of the separation of poetry and prose, of the separation of prose and mathematics. The attempts of our prehistorians to divide man's periods by neo- and paleolith, by iron and brass were useful as long as we did not or could not "hear" these neolithians and paleolithians speak. Prehistory seemed to lack any documents except excavated tools. But our penetration into grammatical structures as revealing the history of a language may increase linguistic documentation of those distant times to sizable proportions.[17]

A third road opens into logic. Much has been said about this in a previous chapter. One of the most practical results of our discussion was the discovery that rational speech presupposes ritualistic speech. We discovered that the logic of our schools covered at best one fourth of the real territory of logic. Before anything can be computed, calculated, observed or experimented with, it must have been something named, spoken to, operated with or experienced. In its generalizations and numerals science strips things of their names. It can do this only with things which were previously dressed in names. Science is a secondary, emancipating approach to reality. We first must have been bound and rooted into a named universe before we can be emancipated by science.

This brief survey of new roads shows that, among the seven liberal arts, the so-called *trivium* of grammar, rhetoric and logic profits most from our studies. Our approach raises the "trivialities" of these three introductory fields of knowledge to the stature of full-grown sciences. They will become the great sciences of the future. This is a rise to power which has its parallel four hundred years ago in the rise of the so-called quadrivium to scientific significance. Before 1500 only theology, law and medicine were the sciences of God, society and body, while the quadrivium (arithmetic, geometry, music, astronomy) and the trivium (grammar, rhetoric, logic) were mere servants and auxiliary tools.

Humanism emancipated arithmetic, geometry, music and astronomy, and replaced medieval medicine by a whole series of sciences on the physical world, including our own bodies. Since 1800 the trivium has stirred too. But mostly it was still treated by the methods of the quadrivium as an appendix of the physical enlightenment. The law faculty needs to be replaced by a whole group of the social sciences, including one about our own consciousness.

A brief example of such an application to our own consciousness may be given here. Our consciousness functions only as long as our minds respond to imperatives and as long as we use metaphors and symbols. Scientists themselves must speak trustingly and confidingly before they can think analytically.

What is a symbol, what is a metaphor that they should be man's daily bread? Symbols are speech crystallized. And speech crystallizes in symbols because in its creative state it is metaphorical. Symbols and metaphors are related like youth and old age of speech.

At first sight, a wedding ring, a coffin or a top hat may seem to exist without language. Are they not mute? Alas, speech has led to these symbols, or they could not be symbols at all!

This is a hard doctrine. But it is universally true. Even the logicians' symbols themselves prove it. "1," "-," "=" are crystallized speech. They make us listen to the logicians because their original speech character is still transparent. Speech must lead to symbols. Symbols result from speech. We "listen" to symbols as though they were speech. We "look" at speech because it will lead to symbols.

Is this a mere play on words?

The first thing that struck me in a coal mine was the importance of the worker's hat for a miner. There he stood, stripped to the waist, blackened, sweating, but with a hat to don when you spoke to him. It seemed to me like an assertion of his being a citizen, an equal to everybody under the sun, although underground he worked like a dumb beast. He wore his hat not as a protection against the sun but as the symbol of a free man's franchise. In the coal mine or on the railroad track, wherever men slave at a wearisome manual task, a hat lies ready to be donned when it's time to speak to another man or to have a drink with other fellows at the bar. A danger is avoided by the hat, the danger that a passing state of animal toil should alter the free status of the human toiler.

With the help of the hat, he remains a free citizen. The harder the toil the more valued the hat. Millionaires and college students can forget about hats.

Symbols represent the "real" or main state of a person against all appearances. They represent my better self in its absence much like the two senators of each state of the Union represent their state at the seat of the central government.

Where wedding rings are worn, the married man is recognized even though he is far from home and although in all other ways his appearance may be that of an adventuresome Don Giovanni. The black dress of a mourner represents his loss despite the fact that he moves in public like anybody else.

This gives us a clue to the authentic places of symbols. They follow acts of investiture by which they have become indelible and important elements of reality. The wedding ring is no good if a husband can put it into his pocket. He must bow to the act which made him wear it or the symbol ceases to be a symbol. The senators can only represent their state in Washington as long as we believe in majority vote and free elections. They must be treated as symbolizing their state because they have been placed in this position by the ritual of an election at home. The wedding ring can only be worn because it has been placed on the finger in a serious ring-ceremony.

A ritual precedes the symbol. If no such ritual has invested the person, the symbol is a mere ludicrous plaything. The power of the symbol depends on the power of the custom in human relations which it represents − in the absence of the custom. The farmers at Lexington and Concord, the rabble in arms who proved the equals of the regular standing army of the British, made the hats of American citizens the symbol of freedom. The scars of battle are sacred. The tattoos of the tribesmen are everlasting symbols of battle prowess. This explains the sham battles of innumerable rituals. They had to invest the initiate with the symbols of courage.

The symbol sticks the better the more seriously the ritual has been "spoken." But there is no symbol without speech. As it has been wisely said of the Declaration of Independence: It gave the Americans for the first time a character, it introduced them to the world as Americans; by the Declaration's solemn act, they ceased, in the eyes of the world, to be British colonists.

Symbols restate the fact that speech aims at long-range truth and that, for this purpose, it seeks to replace the appearances of the visible world by some higher, better or more penetrating order. Since the symbol shows its effectiveness best when the investing ceremony is over, these ceremonies are conceived from the very beginning as a power which creates a second world.

Human speech is metaphorical by establishment. Nothing, in speech, is what it is. Everything means something which in itself it is not. Let us look at some of the evidence. Of an Osage ritual, Francis La Flesche reports:

"The sky mentioned in the ritual here given . . . is not the material sky that surrounds us but the sky of conduct of men toward one another, a sky which might be overcast with dangerous and destructive clouds of war, but which could be influenced by men, through self-restraint, self-denial, and good will which alone can avert the storms of hatred and malice, and make the sky of conduct clear and serene.

"Like other teachings that touch closely the life and welfare of the people, the teaching of peace could not be preserved or transmitted in any other way than by rites. . . . The [singers], in this ritual, chose the sky and the variety of changes it assumes when in a peaceful mood, and the activity of the birds at such times, to illustrate and set forth their teaching of peace. 'The bird who sits as though he had been struck with a tinge of red,' (cardinal) is associated with the soft morning clouds that are struck with a tinge of red by the rising sun, and which promise a calm day. The bluejay with the sky, which although clouded, is serene and shows its color of blue through intervening spaces; the scarlet tanager with the red dawn that is an unfailing sign of a bright day; the spotted duck, with the sky flecked with harmless blue clouds; the 'great Curlew,' with the sunny day, the coming of which he predicts by his cry, even before dawn; and lastly, the white swan, with the sky that is perfect in purity and peace."[18]

That ritual shows the need for metaphor. But this need is greater still when the institutional life of a community must be set off against the natural world. La Flesche reports elsewhere that:

"The 'No$^n$-ho$^n$-zhi$^n$-ga' is the tribal order enacted by all the members on the Buffalo hunt as well as in the religious rites. No ceremony could be performed unless all its parts were represented. The position of each gens in the place of meeting . . . cannot be changed or shifted. The one exception is the case in which a ceremony is performed for the member of one gens. Then this gens sits in the eastern end of the part used for this ceremony. All other gentes, however, remain in their permanent place even then.

"The two divisions represent sky and earth. The sky division 'Tsizhu' is at the north, the earth division 'Honga' is at the south. Sky is divided by day and night, earth in water and land. The Honga Uta nondsi (earth) here counted as 7, counts as the most important, or even as one by itself."[19]

La Flesche provides the following diagram to show these ritual orders:

*Order of Position of Gentes in the Assembly of the Osage:*

F = Fireplace

### NORTH

| 7 | 6 | 5 | 4 | 3 | 2 | 1 |

Tsi-Zhu Dual Division

|  |  | officers |  |
|---|---|---|---|
| WEST | F    F | of the | EAST |
|  |  | ritual |  |

Honga Dual Division

Dry Land Group        Water Group

| 7 | 6 | 5 | 4 | 3 | 2 | 1 | | 7 | 6 | 5 | 4 | 3 | 2 | 1 |

### SOUTH

| *North Side* | *South Side* |
|---|---|
| SKY DIVISION | EARTH DIVISION |
| 1. Sun people | A. Dry Land Group |
| 2. Buffalo face people | 1. Eagle people |
| 3. Elder Sun carriers | 2. Black Bear people |
|    Star people | 3. Puma people |
|    Moon people | 4. Elk people |
| 4. Dawn people - peace gens[20] | 5. Crawfish people |
| 5. Night people | 6. Wind people |
|    Fire people | 7. Earth people |
| 6. Those who came last | |
|    Men of Mystery | B. Water Group |
|    Thunder people | 1. Turtle carriers |
| 7. Buffalo Bull | 2. Meteor people |
| |    Pure watermen |
| |    Peace gens |
| |    Water people |
| |    Cattail people |
| | 3. Deer people |
| | 4. Keepers of the bow |
| | 5. Night and Fish people |
| | 6. Deer people |
| | 7. Hail people |

A new son of the whole tribe is begotten as a reaffirmation of peace and good will, in a great ceremony which draws their villages together in new harmony and assures continuity of the race.

Conception, gestation, birth of a new Honga, the tribe's little one, or son, the new Prince of Peace, are enacted. For instance, in the fourth song, at the last note, the sacred pipes in the hands of the "ritualists" are allowed to slip from their fingers, but before they touch the ground, they are caught up by two other officers. This means: the child is born.

Very wonderful is the selection of the candidate. The two great matrimonial divisions of the tribe, sky and earth, select four candidates each by sticks named after the candidate. Then the wife of the man who is going to perform the ceremony selects the stick of the future "Child of Peace"; by this selection, the wife enables her husband to treat the "child" now as his son and as their common child.[21] The Christmas story is not far removed from this remarkable ritual.[22]

Perhaps one such example may seem to prove nothing. I hold that a single ceremony of one single tribe fully understood and appreciated is more instructive than 1001 aphorisms culled from scattered places.

But by now anthropologists no longer need to be convinced of the power of ritual. It has been found everywhere. The Germanic tribes have not spoken differently from the Osage, the Greeks no differently from the Australians. All speech invests the physical world with a second meaning against appearances: It creates associations which do not exist in the world of the individual's five senses. Speech creates a common sense. Because it is intended to be a sense common to all, it must abstract from any individual's sense perceptions or moods. Speech creates permanent and common associations. And that which our semanticists and logicians contemptuously reject as metaphor, imagery, associative thinking, symbolism or mysticism has associated man with his fellow men in ever increasing societies through the ages.

When we speak, we associate or dissociate. The fallacy of the mind is in the unwarranted optimism that a man can speak his mind, on the one hand, and can associate or dissociate, on the other hand, in two separate procedures. Taking language for granted, as being "native" and "natural" to man, reason has ignored the precarious existence of speech as the lifeblood of the human community. If the speaker denies the community, its lifeblood is spilled. In a tribe speech carried on outside the political order became and becomes witchcraft. Arbitrarily spoken, solemn songs grow hollow and drive people crazy instead of directing their actions.

In our modern world, when speech is denied its precarious political function inside a growing humanity trying to be born, it becomes abstract criticism, debunking, which scents superstition in any form of human speech, election, ritual or symbol. No true scientist is guilty of such abuse of speech. A true scientist builds up the republic of scholars with his contributions. Every science is a fellowship of language and thereby links people in an ever-increasing communion. Science upholds man's eternal faith in the power of speech. Like all other forms of speech, science associates men of good will by creating one common sense above the individual senses, one common nature above the relative natures of separate beings. Science establishes an inner social world against and above the physical world.

Solely Alexandrian traditions of philosophy, grammar and logic have lagged behind the real communal symbolism of science. While in its laboratories science has created new rituals and new symbols, the theories of thought and of science have not yet been emancipated from their Aristotelian, Stoic and Alexandrian ancestors. Thanks to anthropology, this is no longer necessary. Every report from every corner of the world can't help testifying to the ritual of speech. Image, comparison, metaphor, symbol are the conditions of human intercourse. The great words of Greek tragedy were not its trimmings or "poetic" ornamentation, as Gilbert Murray thought in his "poetical" translations of the Greek classics. They were the religious and legal terms by which the Greeks built the common sense of their cities and by which the inner world of their society was made to proceed from the chaos of outer strife.

The notion of poetical language during the Victorian age was strangely unreal. A skeleton of rational and logical thoughts was draped fancifully with "beauty," with the jewelry of similes, old fashioned words of Anglo-Saxon or Greek origin, and this was thought to be "poetry." But this is not the distinction between poetry and prose at all. In a later section on the first human poems, we shall define the true difference between prose and poetry extensively and explicitly.

In this section on the ritual of speech, it only is necessary to refute the Victorian ideas on poetry as using metaphor, and scientific prose as using no metaphor. One might put it both ways: all science is based on metaphor; genuine poetry does not use metaphor in the Victorian sense.

## 12. Grammatical Health

We have to be spoken to lest we go mad or fall ill. The first condition of health is that somebody speak to us with singleness of purpose, as though we were the only one. In her novel *Paradise*, Esther Forbes has a young woman in travail recover miraculously because the lover of her childhood enters the room and talks to her in unique tones which make sense solely between her and him.[23] This relation between our health and being spoken to with the power of our unique "vocative" necessitates resistance against an education solely by the state. Never will a child be at peace which has not meant the world to somebody and has been spoken to as though it were the only child on earth.

The other day a modern psychologist took over a New York kindergarten. The mothers of the children took turns there and they loved the work. The psychologist fell into a rage: she lectured these poor mothers that they were unable to be impartial, that jealousy and envy and complexes would result; she sent them home feeling pretty small, and she subjugated the nursery — children of 3 and 4 years were involved — to the objective psychologist. We are so civilized that nobody beats up such a scoundrel; under modern rules, this psychologist is feted, and the mothers retire bedraggled.

The whole phase of life in which a child listens in rapture to a person's voice who thinks of nobody but him and cares for nobody else quite as much is suppressed by this factory-mentality. The professional psychologist, in their whole game, is himself or herself the only mental case, a power-lusting animal, a beast of prey, grammatically an ego, with the children as objectified "its." All psychology textbooks are marred by the same mistake which marred William James's psychology. At the end of his life James himself confessed that it was based on an error. The foundation of psychology, he said repentantly, is the fact that we wish to be appreciated by others.

Nowadays our textbooks do mention this. But they bring it in belatedly, and it is a mere addition to the previous description of the self by itself.

Twenty-five years ago an old worker on his deathbed told me, "the whole sum of the social question is this: 'man wants to have been loved and to have loved.' – the past perfect of his formula is highly significant – ' and the worker as a worker is not loved by society.' " What James called "appreciation," with modern evasiveness, and what the dying worker Haasis called "love," is grammatically speaking an invocation, directed exclusively at the loved one.

The difference between being patted on the back as a G.I. or as Joe DeVivo, the cook, is tremendous. Love is antinumerical. "Love me" cannot be believed by anybody who does not feel some selective and exclusive meaning behind this challenge. Any educator may impart justice, equity, prudence or fairness. But most educators are trained by psychologists who abhor exclusiveness and proclaim that it is sin to say: "Love me," and, "I love you exclusively." They try to make children live on the second level of general relations before they have experienced the first level of exclusive and personal relations. This prejudice against the exclusive invocation is destroying man's grammatical health. Never do we respond with might and main to a call which does not single us out. The degree of response is in exact proportion to the degree of exclusiveness of the call for us.

The deviltry of the New York psychologist is the same as with all devils: they evade the incarnation of real persons. She did not know that exclusiveness is the basis of a soul's response. She only saw the risk involved of some children being treated better than others in the process. Corruption of the best always is the worst. Nothing is more terrible than a mother who becomes a whore or a genius selling out to Hollywood. Is this a reason to reject motherhood or genius? *Corruptio optimi pessima*, indeed, but the best is still the best. Certainly no psychologist can make the fatal mistakes of a jealous mother. Neither can a professional who deals with dozens and scores of children for a living ever achieve the one quality which even the worst mother has by the grace of God: to speak and to think and to act as though the child were her own.

Ownership often is pretty terrible, but it is the mainspring of all grandeur, too, when it is held in the true and genuine spirit of exclusiveness. This spirit simply consists in the knowledge: "Nobody else will," "I am the only person in the world," "this is the only child in the world." Whoever has this spirit of exclusiveness to another human being has a quality, a "grammatical" quality which nobody else has and which is indispensable. This quality is the quality of giving orders: of saying: listen, come, eat, love me, go to sleep. Others may give such orders in imitating this quality. In an orphanage 160 children may be told to eat, to come, to listen, to go to sleep. But the right to give these orders here is derivative. It is derived from genuine parenthood. The right of giving orders depends on the quality of putting those to whom these orders are given above everything else. A platoon leader who is indifferent to the fact that this is his platoon and that his men must know that he won't give any order without being controlled by this "my-platoon-idea," is disqualified. The person who will never think of passing the buck, who knows that he can't pass the buck, acquires the right to give orders.

Why did the psychologist eliminate the mothers from "her" own kindergarten, the psychology-kindergarten? She could not help doing so and was amply justified in her own eyes. For it is true, a normal mother and her child are ignorant of the two first psychological categories. They are ignorant of both ego and it.

Mothers become conscious of being mothers only in the process of giving orders, singing songs and telling stories to their children. And children become sons and daughters through their mothers' voices. The ritual of speech has its original potency between mother and child. And we have recognized that the potency of any imperative depends on the speaker throwing himself outside himself into the order he gives, and the listener is thrown into action. Both, then, are outward directed, or, as we usually say, they are not self-centered. In the mother's call: "Come, Johnny," the invocation: "Johnny," draws out the mother's self, the verb "come" draws out the child's self. Both surrender to a mutual interaction.

The role of the vocative is understood as little today as that of the imperative. Few people pay any attention to the fact that all languages have special vocatives. There is little doubt for me that our forms Nick, Jack, Jim, are at least partially genuine vocatives. But they are classified by our grammar books and dictionaries as "diminutives," "nicknames," "funny appelations." We thereby suppress our understanding of the vocative as a universal necessity. It seems an accident or a luxury of language. This is not the case. A vocative shows speech at its creative stage because at first we speak not of dead things but to living people. The whole linguistic world of philology thought it normal to start its analysis of language with sentences like "Zeus rains" or "the sun shines" or "the soldiers march," or even worse, with the nominatives Zeus, sun or soldiers. Plato's "Cratylos" is the sad model of this hackneyed approach to speech. How the author of this dialogue can be considered the saint of the liberal arts college is a mystery in itself. Plato certainly had lost touch with his people, for their first approach was not to speak in nominatives but to shout: "Send rain, O Zeus!"

Nobody should believe that this is a play on grammatical forms on my part. Whole nations have been made over by vocatives. The greatest example of this is the City of Rome. In the sixth century this little speck inside the Latin territory rejected the worship of Zeus Veiovis, the little Zeus in his representation as an adolescent and as the God of the netherworld. And evolving their own conceptions, they concentrated on Jupiter, the vocative of Father Zeus. The Latin name was pushed into the background by this vocative of Father Zeus; it withered in the countryside where the family of Julius Caesar officiated for him. The citizens of Rome could look down on those unreformed peasants. And the Romans never had any "nominative case" for their supreme god.[24]

> Rain Zeus; Rain, Jupiter!
> March, soldiers!
> Shine, Sun!
> Be my wife!

is the first layer of speech; in a living universe, appellation and appeal come before nouns.

In our grammar vocatives are listed. It is said that persons addressed are called by this "case". But the wavering between the terms invoke, call, vocative and appellation, address or proper name for this central act already betrays an insecurity. Also the term "invocation" is left apart from "vocative" and "appelative." But vocative and invocation and appeal necessarily belong to each other. The speaker prejects himself upon them. We find ourselves in our vocatives. As the mother becomes a mother by calling her child's name, so do we become officers by calling upon our men, bosses by calling upon our workers, teachers by calling upon our students. The vocatives do something to their speakers. They draw them out. Our vocatives are our faith. Vocatives come before nominatives, whatever our grammarians may say.

The witty French saying *"Je suis leur chef; il faut que je les suive"* is simply true. We are pledged to those whose "head" (*chef*), whose speakers we are, to those who call us in the vocative — and I have personally experienced this in great moments when called upon. He who is ready to abandon himself and put all his faith into another person's name — is drawn out of himself and above himself, he becomes this invoked name's trustee, leader and representative. At the outbreak of war, I was compelled to believe in the voice which defied some 20,000 people in a railway station, a real ocean of excited humanity. The voice shouted my name without embarrassment at the top of his lungs. I had to believe because the person who shouted my name believed in me and revealed it to me in this ocean of excitement.

When Homer invokes the Muse, he does not play with some archaic form, as does a poet of the baroque. Homer loses himself, his own prosaic, non-poetical self in the invocation and grows roots in the poetical field of the Olympian Muses. It may be hard for us to recover this sense of his invocations because we are Alexandrians. But we cannot comprehend the great hour of the birth of poetry unless we see Homer throw himself upon this meadow outside of his everyday self — which he was the first human being to discover.

We inhabit or settle into our vocatives whenever they are genuine. Here is another literary example. The 19th century French made a cult of Athens. Therefore when Count Gobineau composed his medieval *Amadis*, Athens had to be brought in as it was brought in by Clemenceau, by Anatole France, by Flaubert, by innumeable writers. How was this done? Gobineau gives us to understand, by a simple vocative, that his spiritual home is Athens. The verse, and he must have been proud of it, reads: *"Et toi, Athenes, Athenes, Athenes, Athenes,"* quite some vocative. But the soul of the poet enters her true home in the invocation. By a tour de force, Athens is made part of his medieval world.

Juliet, does so too, when she calls Romeo's name. But Shakespeare the omniscient (and from him do I know it) adds the lucid interpretation by Romeo: "It is my soul who calls upon my name." The vocative and the invocation have not gotten their due in linguistics. If they had, the first lines of the Iliad as well as of the Odyssey would have instilled more respect in the negators of their unity. If the invocation had been appreciated as the speaker's invocation of his spiritual homestead, it would have been understood that "wrath" and "man" were the themes the great poet had settled on when invoking the Muse, and that no afterthought ever could evoke the timecup of expectation and fulfillment so perfectly with one single word.

There exists a rather overused term for this form of a speaker's health; we call it "responsibility." But the term has lost its luster since it has been made too active. "Come, Johnny!" is a responsory in which mother and child lose themselves, she by throwing all her weight upon the vocative, he by allowing the imperative to settle on him as the "footstool," the subject of the action. Nobody can be "responsible" without response; it would be too one-sided an existence.[25]

Modern grammar overlooks the fact that all life is ambivalent; it oscillates between active and passive. It must have been "middle voice," before it is more active than passive or more passive than active. We don't make people "responsible" by preaching. They must bathe in the middle voice of solidarity and singleness; the rest will follow. In sentences formed by a vocative plus an imperative, we have the "middle voice" situation (in Greek the medium) pretty clearly. The captain who can say to his men: "Men of Company C, take that village," makes them active as he is activated by throwing himself on their invoked name. The soldiers who take the village are not made "passive" in the grammatical sense because they have heard their captain's order. He is not "active," grammatically speaking. Both are active as well as passive. And this is the human norm. Any unquestioning, unselfconscious, happy and gracious group lives the middle voice in which the division between active and passive remains undeveloped and is less important than the responsory between people who believe in their unique solidarity.

Marriage would be impossible without this correlation between vocative and imperative. Here the speaker lives in the vocative; the listener comes to life in the imperative. The terrifying abuses of "honey, wash the dishes," "darling, shut up," do not refute the great truth of the right usage. A psychologist, however, would abolish marriage, because of its possible failure.

Among grammarians the middle voice is treated as an absurdity of Greek grammar and of the Latin *deponentia*. But it is the language of paradise and innocence, the language of unbroken solidarity.

Another example of grammatical health may be taken from the historical form of speech: If a child is asked, "what did you have for dinner," it should normally answer, "we had cabbage." If it answers, "I had cabbage," we may be sure that something is very wrong at home. Not only should meals be communal experiences in which food is sanctified by sharing, it also seems to be a fact that we tend to "nostrificate," to "uswardize" history and to speak of social events in the plural of majesty: we, our, us. The same mother and child who live the unique situation of "Come Johnny" by vocative and imperative, who single each other out and forget the rest of the world over each other, will narrate this same scene in terms of "we." In retrospect, the mother will even playfully revamp the fact that Johnny obeyed her orders. The report of an incident in which the boy did not obey at first instinctively is very often shaped in the form of "we." The mother will — especially in Johnny's presence — neither say "he came," nor "you came," but she usually says "and in the end, we came!"

"We" is the bliss of history and memory. As long as I must tell my past in terms of "I," I am not reconciled to it. In retrospect, we try to speak generically. A man might say: "Well, I was 17, and I guess at 17 we all act in this manner." Why? I have no a priori theory about any of these grammatical observations. But I find them to be the great laws of human transsubstantiation. Man changes substantially from agenda of the future to acts of the past by going from "thou" in the future to "we" in the past. Nostrification redeems our solitude as pioneers.

Perhaps we crave fellowship and we treat any call from the future as an opportunity for new fellowship. The solitary pioneer goes forward alone, but why would he do so if there were not the possibility of the whole state of Wyoming resulting from his pioneering? The first act is done alone, but in the success story providence always has made the act become common property and common knowledge. The relation between genuine future and genuine history being that of incognito and universal recognition, of full risk and safety, this substantial change is expressed when "thou" is replaced by "we." As long as the act is not done, the greatest possible pressure must be concentrated on one person who is invoked by name. The act does not exist, and therefore all that exists is the recipient's eagerness to perceive this act's inescapable necessity.

Everybody knows that no order is properly given unless one man is made fully responsible for its execution. In retrospect, all this is changed. The ordered act now is detached from the vocative and its agent because in the meantime the act has been "born" and now the agent is no longer under the power of this vocative and is ready to respond to a new one. As long as the act is called "his" act, it has not been absorbed by fellowship, and he has not been delivered of it completely. Vanity may tempt the doer to retain his name's hold on the act too exclusively. Grammatical health will demand his dismissal from any exclusive hold on the act. The doer is also dismissed from further responsibility by this surrender to "we." He may now beget a new imperative.

The other day in taking leave from a visiting friend, I ventured to say on the doorsteps, "Give my love to your wife." I could have bitten off my tongue for this blunder of "my" before "love." I had a sense of frustration for the rest of the day. Were we not a family, a unity, at our house? Why had I not said: "Give our love?" Nobody can speak of "my" love by proxy anyway.

These two positions, then, of the vocative and the narrative may illustrate the term grammatical health. A human being is healthy who is trans-substantiated continuously through the appropriate grammatical forms. It is "healthier" to say to oneself "don't be a fool" than "I am a fool"; it is healthier to say "we have done well" than "I have done well"; it is also healthier to sing "I wished I were free," or "oh that you loved me" than "may they be happy" and similar pious phrases.

The religious, the poetic, the social and the scientific mind all should have their say and their grammatical representation in our souls. We must be *you's* before we can be *I's we's* or *its* to ourselves. We must transsubstantiate and change from one form to another again and again. All *thous* in us have to be buried objectively some day. But there always must be a new appeal, another *thou*, still invoked and surviving all the historical and analyzed *thou's*, *I's*, and *we's*. Death of the soul follows immediately upon the extinction of a man's ability to respond to his calling.

Grammatical health is the health of transsubstantiation, of substantial change. For it is our very substance which is changed when we proceed from vocative to nominative, from appellation to classification. Grammatical health includes the dying away as well as the coming to life of the spirit. Grammatical health accepts the fact that the spirit must die in order to rise again.

Obviously there are great difficulties in such a state of affairs. Whole communities may deny that a specific inspiration ever died. Other communities may deny that any specific inspiration ever can claim authority.

The ancient world was cursed with undying yet dead spirits. Our mechanized world is cursed with unborn, unacceptable inspirations. Two examples which follow (A and B) may illustrate the great pre-Christian problem of undying spirits, and two (C and D) the problem of still born inspirations today.

A. Every four years we elect a President. For the next four years the American Constitution does not allow a President to appeal to the country for a new vote of confidence. He has, holds and retains his power for four years. Should he wish to resign, his vice president would step in, and thereby block the President's direct appeal to the country. In 1938, with World War II at hand, the President felt miserable about the neutrality legislation – and Mr. Hull, our Secretary of State, wept when Senator Borah blocked all reasonable policy. The President could not resign and force the issue of rapid armament on the country by a courageous campaign. Mr. Churchill or any prime minister of another country could have done so.

The American Constitution, in other words, is inflexible; it does not permit a man to extricate the country from the mold into which a quadrennial election has cast it. There is no way of ex-authorizing the result of an election in the United States. The President cannot resign, because the Vice President is his political alter ego. Physically, the President may resign. But the spirit of the platform on which he was elected would linger on in the person of the Vice President. The political intent and meaning of a political shake-up by resignation is not in the power of a President of the United States while it has been one of the most powerful weapons of men like Disraeli, Clemenceau or Briand.

This limitation of a President's power did not seem unreasonable because of the short term of four years. Perhaps, before 1938, there never was a moment where the lack of this power to exauthorize made itself felt. By realizing that this has become serious in our own world crisis, however, we gain insight into the greater handicaps of other times. If we believe in the rigidity of the spirit so much that it cannot be revoked within a period of four years, the ancients did not know how to revoke it at all. The Witches' Sabbath is a great case in point. The old tribal spring ritual was superseded by Christianity. But how could those magic songs of fertility rites ever lose their hold and their power over the souls of men? They could not as long as there was one direct initiate alive. Goethe's Faust, in his *Walpurgisnacht,* caught the last remnants of a tradition which had continued down to 1700. The witches whose burning we bemoan actually believed themselves to be witches. Their witchcraft was the uprooted, delocalized ritual of the pre-Christian order of society.

Clyde Kluckhohn has given us a remarkable monograph on Navaho witchcraft.[26] He has investigated the facts with extreme caution. He too, however, admits that the destruction of the tribal structure placed the old ritual into the hands of uprooted individuals. "Witchcraft" became ritual handled without responsibility because the authority remained when the responsibility was gone. The knowers of the spells could not be ex-authorized.

When the Erinyes were to be reconciled to the asylum created in Athens, Aeschylus described the magic net of their spells first and then let them acquire a new, euphemistic name – they were called the Eumenides. No spell which was ever created could be annihilated – it had to be bent to new meanings.

Witchcraft, then, is the outstanding example of inspiration unable to be objectified and buried after the group to which it gave life ceases to function.

B. The problem of resignation of a ruler, a king, or emperor is the second great problem of "exauthorization." In fact, history connects this term specifically with the forced resignation in 834 A.D. of one emperor – Louis the Pious.

Pagan Roman Emperors who became impossible had to be slain. But Diocletian, at the threshold of Christianity, conceived of the Emperor's office for the first time as an "exauthorizable" one. In 305 A.D. he voluntarily laid down the purple of "Augustus"; when a colleague later implored him to return to power, he spoke contemptuously of the high office: "If you could see the beautiful vegetables which I grow in Spalato, you would not propose this to me."

In his religion Diocletian went back to the times before Caesars had been made Gods. He was an old Roman of the Republic and he said so: "To my pious and religious mind it seems that the institutions created by the laws of Rome must be respected in eternal religion. I do not doubt that the immortal gods shall continue to favor and protect the Roman name if this pious and religious, quiet and chaste life continues." No "immortal" god wrote this, but a modest man.

By this deliberate reaction, he stepped outside the magic square in which the divinity of a Caesar had been contained. Diocletian who persecuted the Christians for the last time, anticipated the first claim of the new faith in his own practice: that Caesar was a mortal man. In this sense, Diocletian was a real Christian, and Constantine who succeeded him and became the first Christian emperor was less Christian in his practice. The tragedy of the Diocletian persecution consisted in just this fact: that Christians in his reign lusted for power, and he, Diocletian, did not. His enemies have distorted his history, but they did realize his dilemma of *exauctoratio*. "When Diocletian saw that his name was deleted in his own lifetime – something that had befallen no other emperor – he decided to die." (Lactantius 42). *Exauctoratio*, abdication, is impossible while the inspiration is believed to be bona fide.

In the United States election is considered an inspired act; for this reason, no President can make the election result expire before the term is over. But through his archaic Republican-like retirement Diocletian dissolved the inspirational spell cast by the divine name of Caesar Augustus; like a Cincinnatus he returned to the soil. Hence, it was not much for Constantine to conclude that Caesars might become Christians after all. The greatest obstacle to his baptism, lifetime divine inspiration, had been eliminated by the persecutor Diocletian!

Five hundred years later, the bishops of Gaul tried to divest the Emperor of his rank. They divested him of his sword and belt as a warrior, they made him sign a declaration of *exauctoratio*. It was in vain. The people did not believe that an annointed ruler ever ceased to be the right ruler. They had to reinstate him. At the end of this same ninth century, the Witches' Sabbath broke loose in the papacy itself. That is to say, the Pope himself appeared to those teutonized churchmen as wielding eternal irrevocable magic. Pope Formosus had been transferred from one bishopric to another in Dalmatia and during a short reign had consecrated priests in Rome. His enemies wished to prove that a bishop could not be transferred from one see to another without invalidating his office – a rule which was indeed an old sacrament of the church. Hence, they dug his corpse from the grave, put him on his throne, held a regular trial against the corpse, cut off his hand, and by eliminating the hand which had done the consecrating, they convinced themselves that his acts now were null and void. The difficulty of voiding his authority seemed so unsurmountable that he had to lose his carnal hand before the spell was felt to have been broken! But we may pause to respect the difficulty in which these poor people found themselves when we see that the Navaho Indians were on the verge of killing each other by witchcraft and the resulting anarchy of "spells" had not the American Government intervened.[27]

And now let us look at the opposite difficulties of our own world: too early reflection on creative actions.

C. In my own experience, two enterprises to which I was dedicated were wrecked by premature publicity. No imperative can thrive unless it receives its first exclusive response through action before generalizing reflection and public exposure sets in. The lighted "time cup" of a command must be rounded out by fire and warmth before the first objective analysis sets in, or the field of force inside of which a group can cooperate will never come into existence. In one of the two cases, the little man who destroyed our work was implored not to write us up too early. He had the chance of making some money out of us by an article for the *New York Herald Tribune*. His article mobilized the merely curious four weeks too early, and we were annihilated. The man thought that by praising us he could minimize the harm. Praise or criticism are equally destructive in such a case of premature publicity.

I could give many more details. My own causes may seem too personal to be analyzed here. The great war effort of the whole country is a better case; the course of events is clear enough. By the fall of 1944, the imperative "War" had nearly exhausted its spellbinding force. Governor Dewey campaigned for President under the slogan: "The war will be over on January 20, 1945 when I am to be inaugurated." An imperative ceases to work when we look beyond its completion. First things come first. Whenever a human soul is not contained in the time cup of such an indubitable "first thing," she ceases to be able to give her very best to its fulfillment. People withdrew from factory work. Between October and Christmas 1944 five of my own friends stopped their participation in the war effort, each one for a different reason. But reasons are as plentiful as blackberries when the spell of a time cup evaporates. The election-spell interfered with the war spell. Both spells are and should be effective spells. Here they collided. This does not mean that any society can live without them.

D. Jobs in our factories and the marriages of our divorcing humanity are, of course, the individual similes of the "limited" effort for the war. The simple fact that people assume divorce is possible wrecks many marriages. The last effort is not made to fulfill the vow of a marriage when we can look beyond it. Especially a woman threatened by the husband's changing desires must behave very differently from a normal wife. A friend of ours who loved her husband passionately and had two children by him, saw him run away with another woman. She had no place to go; her heart forbade her to stay in the same city with him. She moved to the place where she had been in a summer camp as a child for three summers. In her unpreparedness, this was the only residence she could think of. Shrewder women foreseeing such agony will cultivate friends, localities, activities outside the matrimonial field before the worst has happened. They will wish to have something to "fall back" upon, in case . . . but this means a withholding of faith, energy and devotion from marriage. It makes the marriage one enterprise among others. The vicious circle is on. Being treated as a relative task, marriage will become of only relative importance. Once it is of relative importance, it can end as all relative things do. And simply because of this it will come to an end.

Any plural will kill growth. Our fear of absolutes often prevents us from protecting growth; no first thing can be fulfilled when it is treated as one thing among others. We said that numerability is the achievement of the cooling off mood of the *indicativus abstractus,* of the nameless speech of all analysis: "this is just one case of matrimony; this is one war among others; this is one plan among many." Numerating cannot be admitted into any process of growth. It breaks the spell of the time cup; it strips the soul of her ritual of speech. And then the soul remains stunted. Most of our young workers have lived as stunted souls since all their jobs were simply "job twenty-three" or "thirty-four," and therefore they meant nothing in their lives.

The exauthorization of spells and the reverence for the time cup are both the main tasks of grammatical health. We shall fall sick from both the failure to end and the mistake of beginning at the end with reflection and classification.

A healthy soul speaks of itself as *thou* religiously, as *I* poetically, as *we* socially, as *it, he* or *she* scientifically in the proper rhythm of its fulfillment. The soul cannot begin with *it* nor end with *thou* or *we*. Ever since our society has tried to persuade the "public" that it is an *it, id est*, the public has ceased to be the people who are moved by the spirit from faith through song and experience to knowledge, from first things to last things, from their calling to their incarnation. The souls of many Navaho Indians remain spellbound by witchcraft. The souls of many young Americans remain stunted from lack of grammatical health!

## 13. Genus (Gender) and Life

The speech of mankind is the speech of men and women about the world, and therefore three elements are always involved. The constant proposing and courting of women by men's words, names, gifts and household money, and the constant wielding of authority, administering of order and education, and handling of supplies, by women finds expression in the gods and goddesses of religion and the two genders of grammar.

The two grammatical forms have more in common than we recognize at first sight. It is a wise thing that grammar does not speak of sex but of gender. For gender does not ascribe the titles "he" or "she" to bodies on the basis of mere sex. A ship and a car may be she, and the Church and Europe may be so called; and at other times cars, churches and continents may be spoken of as "it." By this simple fact gender suggests a greater comprehensiveness than could a division by anatomical sex organs only. Gods and goddesses, on the other hand, descend from the sky of lofty divisions in heaven. "Zeus" and earth, "Gaea," split into Jupiter and Juno, Freya (Friday) and Wodan (Wednesday), and thereby get down to the earthly level of bisexual humanity. We do not understand gender or gods unless we perceive that at the outset, male and female sex is employed by speech to hint at more universal divisions than just male and female in the physiological sense.

It is the same with gender as with all grammar. As we have seen, corporeal things were ceremoniously used to make us enter the gates of ritual and change our minds. Crowns, beads, garlands, staffs or shoes were put on or laid off so that we might enter a more lasting realm than each body's senses could experience. Through the gates of a ritual a youth entered his destiny; and therefore he put on a loincloth on the other side of the gate, lest he forget his lasting role from the day of initiation onward. Through all the vicissitudes of youth, maturity and old age — sickness and health, peace and war, at home and alone in deserts, exile and captivity — his loincloth went with him and his name went too. Fifty or sixty years were cut out by one name as a time continuum, with a definite beginning in the act of initiation and a definite end in burial. People buried their dead because socially, in the realm of the spirit, the end of the loincloth was more important than the end of the man's physical body. At the funeral the man's tattoos, clothes, and armor were buried; for sixty years they had been the standard-bearers of the man in his battle for life within the realm of society, in the hunting grounds and villages and assemblies of his tribe. They sealed him into the deliberately created space and time, country and period, of which he had become a member.

Grammatical gender plays a part in this entrance through the gates of ritual into the Elysian fields of lasting order. Our pronominal distinction nowadays between *she*s, *its* and *he*s is, of course, a small residue of gender in its full form in high ritual. Nevertheless, even this residue seemed so fundamental to recent Scottish theology that the dogma of the Trinity was declared necessary since God had to be he, she, and it, in order to be all in all.

However, consideration of the grammatical wealth of gender in pre-Christian speech might be more convincing than this speculation. Astonishingly, nearly any word in Greek or old-Germanic could be turned into a masculine, a feminine or a neutral form. The Greek word for army could be *stratos* (m.), *stratia* (f.) or *strateuma* (n.). In many cases we are led to believe that "originally" the distinction of gender was employed not for male, female and "neuter" but divided "animate" and "inanimate objects" only. On the other hand, it has been held that males and females had their classificatory endings, but the *its* had none and were developed much later into a class. Moreover, in African languages, more than three classes do occur.

If we are faithful to our principle that every possibility and every variety within a given horizon of social integration must have been tried by mankind on each rung of the ladder which reaches down from today into the past of our race, we should expect to find all the existing variation in genders of grammar — and in gods and goddesses. But the necessity to express gender at all on all these many pathways of grammatical classes and forms is a truth we find in our own mind too. And from this, our own calamity or privilege gives us the right to declare that gender is a fundamental category of speech and that it does not intend to describe sex. All languages are compelled by the very situation in which we speak to have some way of expressing gender. And in no languages did "gender" impart the anatomical fact of sex but employed sex as a symbol of the roles in speech and parlance. As we all speak to somebody else about something, the male sex was employed as preponderantly speaking, the female as preponderantly receptive, the neuter as preponderantly talked about.

Perhaps *father* and *mother* received their very names for this reason. Both words, "fa-ther" and "mother," are comparatives like "other," "bet-ter," "big-ger." The father is "more of" a father than the mother; the mother "more of" a mother than the father. Sister and brother are similarly structured. Above we clumsily labelled the situation of male, female and neuter as being preponderantly actively speaking, preponderantly receptively listening, and preponderantly narrated. Well, the word "preponderantly" is worked into the structure of the words "father" and "mother." The father listens, too; and the mother speaks as much as he. Yet it is profoundly true that a name is a weight. We speak for emphasis. One name given, one definite order set, protects a woman for ever. Names command respect, they enforce manners. Definite names make all words last. The qualities of gods and goddesses are distributed in the same manner throughout the gentile world. The creating and the conserving, the sudden and the lasting, the aggressive and the protective, the loud initiative and the quiet throb of the universe — all these are gods and goddesses. For this reason it seems a misnomer to divide the classes of gender into "animate" and "inanimate" objects. There are no animate objects. The division is into subjects and objects. To be animated means to be a subject. We split into those who participate in animated conversation and the objects which do not.

In tribal associations men made peace in their great nominal covenants and thereby created the "pronominal" families in which women had protection from rape. Gender reflects this fact of stormy, excited festivals and rhythmical daily life. Those who spoke at assemblies were of one gender. Those who stayed behind, or only listened, were of the other; those who did not participate at all were of a third kind.

This distinction, we may suppose, was fundamental to us. If I analyze "What is God?," I shall never be able to prove anything but "the divine" quality, or "being," i.e. something in the inanimate object category. Analysis speaks of things as though they can't listen in. Theology analyzes God as though he did not listen in at this very moment. As a result the divine of neutral gender as an inanimate object is the theme of theology. Theology as the science of knowing God is at odds with faith in God, the unknowable.

There are two other treatments. Poetically I may speak of "the Deity." This potentially allows her to live. I am reverent, although I don't expect her to speak. Nature, science or the navy may be treated as deities, that is as "she's." I am also using the category of listening subject, tentatively, when I say "she" of my ship or my car.

But when I dare to use the word God really and fully, I must take the risk of blaspheming, of using his name in vain, of seeing myself penalized by his sudden intervention. For in this case of saying "God," I mean to express my faith in his power of speaking to me. "God," "Deity," "divine," may be com-pared to the three Greek genders for an army. As *stratos*, it is the nation who is sovereign, assembled on the field and ready to legislate. As *stratia*, it is the army, the mistress of her generals, the unit ready to receive their orders and to respond by obedience and discipline. A *strateuma* it is the body of men visibly spread out there in the field, leaders and men, count-able before the spectator's eyes.

Sex, then, is transformed into grammatical gender because the fury and hatred of men was conquered by the names of peace. Should we now start a social cycle in which the jealousies and rancor of women play first fiddle, we may have to change "gender" and call the women "he's" and "they's," and the lovable boys whom these women covet, "she's." The social situation might change. The great tasks of speech would remain unaltered: to differentiate between those who dare to state the terms and names of peace and those who make bold to live them, between the dramatic hero of history and the undramatic heroine of society. For without the undramatic mothers and daughters, the dramatic men would never establish any permanent temporal or geographical organization. Somebody must do what has been said, must wage peace after peace is concluded. And not only that: there must be one half of society who make this "doing what has been said" their predominant business. The term "preponderantly" is a term of reality. Some people have to be more interested in keeping the peace than in waging the next war, just as others will have to keep about abolishing the next injustice, by giving it a stigma, a name which pillories and outlaws it.

Gender is an eternal category in the battle for justice. For all laws must be kept, and all laws must be broken, and all laws must be replaced by better ones. The mothers preponderantly keep the laws, the sons break them preponderantly. The daughters induce us to rethink our laws. The fathers write new laws.

In the quaint language of the law, the god-like position of the king is expressed in the phrase: Rex can prosecute Smith, Brown and Robinson. Smith, Brown and Robinson cannot prosecute Rex. Rex is without an accusative. This then is the highest parallel to God. God is invoked: Jupiter, as an eternal vocative. The legislator, the king, cannot be accused of breaking a law. He makes the laws. Neuters always appear in the accusative; the alleged nominative of a neuter does not exist. The king and the god only appear in the nominative, genetive or the dative, never in the accusative. God has to become Man before he can be put in the accusative and can be spoken of.[28] Gender is the interplay of speaker and doers of "the word," of revolutionary act and evolution, of sudden and gradual process, of today and always, in the life of speech. Mouth and ear mastered, speaking and listening reconciled – that is the ambitious aim of gender in grammar.

The devil created a third sex. Our grammar books talk of neuter as a third sex. But in the world of animate bodies there are only two sexes. Neuter is without sex, not a third sex. This conclusion may appear silly but it is very important. Today objective science treats us all as neuters, as creatures without mouths or ears. The psychologists and sociologists speak about me as though I had no mouth which I can use at any moment, nor ears which hear what they say about me. For them I am a neuter.

Mankind has always spoken about things without mouth or ears. Especially at work we must discuss our tools, our purposes and plans. Our work, our craft and our tools are appropriately without gender because they have neither mouth nor ears. They are things. Neuters are common in the world. For this reason the Greeks correctly gave the bathtub a pre-Greek name and we speak of automobiles, telephones, and kilometers to participate in the labor of the world.

Genders are the carriers of life. Neuters are foodstuffs and instruments. The earless and mouthless object always leads to a special form of speech. The languages of the Gods and of objects are totally different, yet both are essential, like celebrating and working. The non-gender allows us to study the secret of gender. A tool is without present *(Gegenwart)*. Therefore we call it a thing *(Gegenstand)*. But I can only witness in the present. Witnessing and living witness, gender and speech, create the times.

## 14. Editor's Postscript

*As was mentioned in the Introduction, the manuscript for this book was written at different times and never edited for publication by the author himself. Hence it has some of the characteristics of a series of fragments. Therefore readers may find the following conclusion, which summarizes the book's argument, helpful.*

Speech begins with vocatives and imperatives. It begins with formal speech which moves men to action and is embodied in ritual. Our grammar books on the other hand begin with the nominative and the pronoun *I*. The nominative is only usable when an experience is over. I can only respond as an *I* after I have been addressed as a *thou*. *I* is the last pronoun a child learns to use.

We discovered that our systems of formal logic are skewed by accepting this distortion of our grammarians. The beginning vocative and lyric stages of all experience are thus called illogical even though they are essential before the narrative and nominative (abstract) modes can be applied. Common sense or daily talk is a derivative of formal speech.

Gender identifies the required participants in living interaction and is not synonymous with sex. Neuter is not a third sex but refers to all dead things. Thus grammar is a mirror of the stages of human experience. Inspiration through a vocative or imperative addresses us as a *thou*, then forces us to respond as an *I*, makes us report as a *we*, and at the end a story speaks of us as *they*. Thus we are conjugated through the stages of experience.

Instead of mental health, we propose grammatical health. Grammatical health requires the ability to command, the ability to listen, the ability to act, and finally the ability to free ourselves from the command by telling our story. Only then are we ready to respond again. We demonstrated that grammatical ill health can lead to war, dictatorship, revolution and crisis — and showed how formal speech can overcome these four.

We used the image of a time cup created to be fulfilled and to be discarded in time. All social order depends on the power of invoked names to create a neverending series of such time cups.

The grammatical method does not supply a rule book for our behavior but a method to help us understand our history, to differentiate between valid and invalid names, and to determine the response appropriate to the stage of a particular experience or event. It should create a whole series of new social sciences unhampered by our skewed logic which has been dominated by nominatives and *I*'s.

Grammatical experience changes us. In the world of today, there are people at many different stages of grammatical development, and our method offers them the hope of more successful cooperation and understanding. It gives us all a common history, a history aware of timing, and a foundation for a possible peace among men.

# Notes

1 Heinrich Maier, *Psychologie des emotionalen Denkens* (Tübingen: J.C.B. Mohr (Paul Siebeck) 1908), p. 9.

2 Gothic, Latin, Greek, Lithuanian, Russian, Polish, Czech, Serbian, Celtic, Armenian, Persian, Sanscrit, Icelandic, Swedish, Danish, Dutch, French, German, English, Italian, Spanish, Portugese, and all other Indoeuropean languages. All semitic languages: Hebrew, Syrian, Arabian, Egyptian. Fifteen Ugro-Finnic languages. Twenty African languages.

3 Jakob Waickernagel (1853-1938), Albert Debrunner (1884-1958), Ferdinand Sommer (1875-1962).

4 Some critics, as I am well aware, insist that the Prometheus Pyrophoros was the first instead of the third part of the trilogy on the Titan. They are refuted by the one line we have of this play in which it is said the myriads had bound Prometheus. This could not be said in advance of the play which we have, *Prometheus Bound*, since the binding takes place in this tragedy. Modern criticism, however, thinking that a whole play could not be devoted to the description of how a new cult was introduced, simply corrected our tradition of the line and changed "have bound him" into "are going to bind him." This shows the whole bias of modern criticism, which thinks that cults are uninteresting in drama. In *Eumenides*, however, Aeschylus ends his trilogy on exactly the same key: the Furii receive a temple, and these old goddesses are reconciled to the new gods by this place for them within the city. The Furii call themselves "the old," and violently accuse the new gods of the city! *Prometheus* forms a complete pendant to this solution in the *Eumenides*. Compared to Zeus, his cult among men is new; at the same time, he is not a god as primeval as the tribal powers of vendetta. To give him a cult in Athens did not reconcile tribe and city, but individuality and city. But the problem was equally serious and complex, and certainly as worthy of a whole play as the atonement of the Furii.

5 Maier, *Psychologie des emotionalen Denkens*.

6 The plural endings of the first person should be analyzed in light of this.

7 For Hindus, the imperative is the "best" sentence. "Bring the cow!", the Hindu grammarian says, has authority. It has *akansa, yughata, samnidi* (influence, usefulness, order).

8 Francis La Flesche, *War Ceremony and Peace Ceremony of the Osage Indians* (Smithsonian Institution, Bureau of American Ethnology, Bulletin 101) Washington: U.S. Government Printing Office, 1939, p. 213 f.

9 Maier, *Psychologie des emotionalen Denkens*.

10 Interesting in this respect, Sir Everard F. Im Thurn, *Among The Indians of Guiana* (London: Kegan Paul, Trench & Co., 1883; repr. New York: Dover, 1967), p. 193 f.

11 Alfred Ernest Crawley, *Dress, drinks and drums; further studies of savages and sex*, ed. by Theodore Besterman (London: Methuen & Co., 1931), pp. 54 and 73.

12 From *Social Psychology*, Elinberg.

13 Section 3.

14 Alfred Louis Kroeber, *Zuni kin and clan* (New York: The Trustees, 1917).

15 La Flesche, *War Ceremony and Peace Ceremony of the Osage Indians.*

16 Eugen Rosenstock-Huessy, *Magna Carta Latina* (Pittsburgh: Pickwick Press, 1975).

17 I am familiar with Pater Wilhelm Schmidt's attempts in this direction. Only they seemed to me too atomistic, too much taken at random; every language is one political whole and must be analyzed as a whole, not simply for one feature – which might not even be indigenous. (Wilhelm Schmidt, *Die Sprachfamilien und Sprachenkreise der Erde.* Heidelberg: C. Winder, 1926).

18 La Flesche, *War Ceremony and Peace Ceremony of the Osage Indians.*

19 Ibid., p. 202; the figure showing the positions of the gentes is on page 203.

20 "Dawn" reconciles the war between Day and Night in the Egyptian ceremonial as here.

21 La Flesche, *War Ceremony and Peace Ceremony of the Osage Indians*, pp. 212 ff.

22 Compare Eduard Norden, *Die Geburt des Kindes, Geschichte einer religiösen Idee* (Leipzig, B.G. Teubner, 1924).

23 Esther Forbes, *Paradise* (New York: Harcourt Brace & Co., 1937).

24 "Hercules" is a vocative, too. The Mamertins were called by this name because they invoked Mars iteratively (Mars Mars, Mar-Mar) W. Schulze, *Zeitschrift für Vergleichende Sprachwissenschaft*, pp. 32, 195 A.1 and in *Festschrift* Jakob Wackernagel zur Vollendung des 70. *Lebensjahres am 11. Dezember 1923, gewidmet von Schülern, Freunden und Kollegen.* Göttingen: Vandenhoeck und Ruprecht, 1923.

25 In the *Handbook of Indian Languages*, E. Sapir gives interesting material on responding vocatives between family relations (Edward Sapir, *The Takilina Language of South-Western Oregon* (Franz Boas, *Handbook of American Indian Languages*, Part 2 - Smithsonian Institution, (U.S.) Bureau of American Ethnology, Bulletin 40. Washington: U.S. Government Printing Office, 1922, pp 1-296). here p. 232 ff; similarly Trachtenberg (Lev J. Trachtenberg, *Coos* (ibid. pp. 303-430), here p. 366; Meinhof reports that vocatives lose the suffix of gender (Carl Meinhof, *Der Korandialekt des Hottentotischen* (Berlin: D. Reimer (E. Vohsen), 1930.)

26 Clyde Kluckhohn, *Navaho Witchcraft*, Papers of the Peabody Museum of American Archaeology and Ethnology (Harvard University, XXII, No. 2, Cambridge, Mass.: The Museum 1944).

27 Kluckhohn, *Navaho Witchcraft*, p. 62b.

28 Jane Lane (pseudonym of Elaine Daker) *King James the Last* (London: A. Dakers Ltd., 1942 p. VI.

# Selected Bibliography

This bibliography is a selective listing of books by or relating to Eugen Rosenstock-Huessy. All books in English are currently available (except one noted) and may be ordered, at prices listed, from Argo Books, Norwich, Vermont 05055. Add 10% for postage and handling in U.S., 20% other countries. Prices listed are expected to be valid through 1983. Argo catalog is free on request.

## I. Books by Rosenstock-Huessy in English

*The Christian Future.* Harper, 1966. 306 pp., Paperback $6.95.

*The Fruit of Lips.* Pickwick, 1978. 143 pp., Paperback $4.25.

*I Am an Impure Thinker.* Argo, 1970. 206 pp., Hardbound $10.00; Paperback $6.95.

*Judaism Despite Christianity.* University of Alabama Press, 1969. 198 pp. Hardbound $12.95.

*Magna Carta Latina.* Pickwick, 1974. 296 pp., Paperback $5.25.

*The Multiformity of Man.* Argo, 1973. 78 pp., Paperback $3.50.

*The Origin of Speech.* Argo, 1981. 160 pp., Paperback $6.50.

*Out of Revolution.* Argo, 1969. 795 pp., Paperback $12.00.

*Planetary Service.* Argo, 1978. 144 pp., Paperback $6.00.

*Rosenstock-Huessy Papers, Vol. I.* Argo, 1981. 245 pp., Hardbound $27.00; Plastic-bound Paperback $18.00.

*Speech and Reality.* Argo, 1970. 201 pp., Hardbound $10.00; Paperback $6.95.

## II. Books Relating to Rosenstock-Huessy in English

Gardner, Clinton C., *Letters to The Third Millennium.* Argo, 1981. 272 pp., Hardbound $12.95; Paperback $7.95.

Preiss, Jack J., *Camp William James.* Argo, 1978. 272 pp., Hardbound $12.00; Paperback $7.00.

Stahmer, Harold, *"Speak That I May See Thee!",* Macmillan, 1968. 304 pp. (Currently out of print.)

III. Books by Rosenstock-Huessy in German

*Das Alter der Kirche.* (Mit Joseph Wittig.) Berlin: Lambert Schneider, 1927-28, 3 Vols., 1,250 pp.

*Das Arbeitslager.* Jena: E. Diedrichs, 1931, 159 pp.

*Das Geheimnis der Universität.* Kohlhammer, 1958, 320 pp.

*Der Atem des Geistes.* Frankfurt: Verlag der Frankfurter Hefte, 1951, 294 pp.

*Der Unbezahlbare Mensch.* Herder, 1964, 173 pp.

*Des Christen Zukunft.* Siebenstern, 1965, 350 pp.

*Die Europäischen Revolutionen und der Charakter der Nationen.* Kohlhammer, 1961, 584 pp.

*Die Hochzeit des Krieges und der Revolution.* Würzburg: Patmos, 1920, 306 pp.

*Dienst auf dem Planeten.* Kohlhammer, 1965, 176 pp.

*Die Sprache des Menschengeschlechts,* Bd. I. Lambert Schneider, 1963, 810 pp.

*Die Sprache des Menschengeschlechts,* Bd. II. Lambert Schneider, 1964, 903 pp.

*Die Umwandlung.* Lambert Schneider, 1968, 140 pp.

*Frankreich-Deutschland.* Vogt, 1957, 108 pp.

*Heilkraft und Wahrheit.* Stuttgart: Evangelisches Verlagswerk, 1952, 215 pp.

*Herzogsgewalt und Friedensschutz.* Neudruck der Ausgabe Breslau 1910. Scientia, 1969. 205 pp.

*Im Kampf um die Erwachsenbildung.* Leipzig: Quelle & Meyer, 1926, 240 pp.

*Industrierecht.* Berlin: H. Sack, 1926, 183 pp.

*Ja und Nein.* Lambert Schneider, 1968. 180 pp.

*Königshaus und Stämme.* Scientia, 1965, 418 pp.

*Soziologie-Bd. I. Die Übermacht der Räume.* Kohlhammer, 1956, 336 pp.

*Soziologie-Bd. II. Die Vollzahl der Zeiten.* Kohlhammer, 1958, 774 pp.

*Werkstattaussiedlung.* Berlin: J. Springer, 1922, 286 pp.

*Zurück in das Wagnis der Sprache.* Vogt, 1957, 82 pp.

# Index

*The words origin and language have not been indexed, the word speech only in special combinations.*